HE TURNED MY SHAME INTO PRAISE

Written by: Beth Lynch

ROYSTON Publishing

BK Royston Publishing
Jeffersonville, IN 47131
http://www.bkroystonpublishing.com
bkroystonpublishing@gmail.com

© 2024

All Rights Reserved. No part of this book may be reproduced, stored in a retrieval system, or transmitted by any means without the written permission of the author.

Cover Design: Bradley Knox
Cover Photography: Beth Lynch

ISBN-13: 9780578711683

Amplified Bible (AMP) - Copyright © 2015 by The Lockman Foundation, La Habra, CA 90631. All rights reserved.

English Standard Version (ESV) - The Holy Bible, English Standard Version. ESV® Text Edition: 2016. Copyright © 2001 by Crossway Bibles, a publishing ministry of Good News Publishers.

King James Version (KJV) – Public Domain

The Message (MSG) - Copyright © 1993, 2002, 2018 by Eugene H. Peterson

New American Standard Bible (NASB) - New American Standard Bible®, Copyright © 1960, 1971, 1977, 1995, 2020 by The Lockman Foundation. All rights reserved.

New International Version (NIV) - Holy Bible, New International Version®, NIV® Copyright ©1973, 1978, 1984, 2011 by Biblica, Inc.® Used by permission. All rights reserved worldwide.

New King James Version (NKJV) - Scripture taken from the New King James Version®. Copyright © 1982 by Thomas Nelson. Used by permission. All rights reserved.

New Living Translation (NLT) - *Holy Bible*, New Living Translation, copyright © 1996, 2004, 2015 by Tyndale House Foundation. Used by permission of Tyndale House Publishers, Inc., Carol Stream, Illinois 60188. All rights reserved.

Printed in the United States of America

Table of Contents

Author's Disclaimer	v
Foreword - Pastor Caroll Clark	vii
Introduction	ix
Acknowledgements	xvii
Chapter 1-My Childhood	**1**
Chapter 2- My Marriage	**35**
Chapter 3- My Lack Of Trust	**71**
Chapter 4- Strongholds	**77**
Chapter 5- Anger	**83**
Chapter 6- Anxiety	**91**
Chapter 7-Unforgiveness	**101**
Chapter 8-Insecurities	**105**
Chapter 9-Purging	**111**
Chapter 10-Forgiveness	**113**
Chapter 11-Unwavering Faith	**117**
Chapter 12-Worth	**125**

AUTHOR DISCLAIMER

People and incidents in this book are composites created by the author from her life experiences. Names and details of the stories have been changed, and similarity between the names and stories of individuals described in this book to individuals known to readers is purely coincidental.

FOREWORD

When I was asked to write the Foreword for Beth's book. I readily said, "Yes." For I have been witness to deep transformation that I must not deny. Beth in this book has left nothing out, spared no transparency to experience her journey.

Honestly, I have to tell you that I missed her horrifying childhood, but I have been a witness to most of her adulthood. It has been a journey of heartache and pain, that only with her love and trust in God, could bring her through.

In this book you will see pain and horrible situations that are almost too much for anyone to endure. However, you will also prayerfully see no matter what you go through, trusting in God will bring you out with the Victory! As Proverbs 3:5 expresses to us.

God has brought Beth from a caterpillar to what is slowly and surely becoming a beautiful butterfly. It is a joy to see how far she has come, and that she is truly ready, willing, and with her (continual) walk with God, able to be an instrument of great use in God's hand and to God's people.

It's exciting to have known and still apart of this beautiful transformation to God's Glory!

I believe as you read the wonderfully, transparent book you will gain hope and delivered from yourself and others.

God bless you as you're with and expecting an open mind read this riveting book!

Pastor Caroll Clark

ACKNOWLEDGEMENTS

God has placed so many people in my life along the way. I will start off with a few teachers that were instrumental in my life.

Susan Kollmeyer was my home economics teacher. I was going through at this time in my life. She once said to me, "If you don't like yourself, no one else can." This is a true statement. Then I didn't understand this, but I do now. Susan, I thank you for your words of encouragement and for being a support to me during this time in my life.

Shirley Henson was the amazing librarian. She was always chipper, helpful, smiling, caring, and kind to me. I so appreciate you for this. It meant a lot to me. You were a support to me as well. Your light just shined, and I knew you were a gem.

There was another teacher who impacted my life as well. His name is Dan Schunks my music teacher. I will tell you how he has been a blessing to me. For some people it might not be such a big deal, but for me at that time it was. In passing, as he was coming down the stairs at school, he would have a newspaper and roll it up and conk me on the head and tell me to smile. It helped for a moment. I knew he cared. I was so broken back then; I didn't know how to live the life I needed to. I thank him for that. I thank you all for being so kind to me.

I had a neighbor who would take me to church with her. She would listen to me, let me talk, and get things out. She had my back. I thank her for that. I love her for being so good to me. I am truly blessed. I love you, sweet lady. I love and appreciate you all for being so kind and caring.

Then God blessed me with a couple who took me in their home for a while. When I lived with them, it was the first time I had ever felt peace. I was able to sleep a whole night through and they are still in my life. I thank God for them. They loved me unconditionally, still do. They have never given up on me. They loved me through my mess. Trust me, I was a mess. I thank them for allowing me to be a part of the family and still being there for me. I love you all so much.

Along the way God has blessed me with others in my life who are near and dear to my heart.

Bishop David Knox, Jr., and First Lady Bobbie Knox have taught me so much. They have always been in my corner and never given upon me. The First Lady has always taught us that you can't live any better than you know. Bishop David Knox, Jr., has always cared about me. He has always taught us in church to read the Word. He would say, "Don't take my word for it! Read it for yourself." He always challenged us. He always loved us. Never spoke a harsh word a day in his life that I recall. I have great admiration for Bishop David Knox, Jr., and First Lady Bobbie Knox. I love you both so much. Thank you for being in my life.

Pastor Caroll Clark has been in my corner when I wasn't in my own corner at times nor anyone else's corner, for that matter. She has been an encouragement to me. She has prayed for me. Really prayed for me. We have had our ups and downs, but at the end of the day love abides. We are very close. I thank God for you Pastor Caroll Clark, for all of your wisdom, prayers, talks, kindness, and love that you have shown me over the years. I love you and thank God for you.

Tyra and Samuel Knox — I love them so much. I call them the "power couple." I admire the both of them. I call Tyra my sister peep, friend, mentor and Samuel my older brother. They have been a support to me on this journey, as well. Brother Samuel thank you for everything and you as well, Tyra. They have been in my corner as well. They have supported me on this journey. They are truly an amazing couple. I thank God for them both.

Bradley Knox designed my book cover. Thank you for using your gift of design. He has my heart, too. I have known Bradley since he was two years old. He is such a great young man. Always sweet to me. Bradley, I thank you for all you do.

Amanda Darden, you know I love you. You have been a support to me for many years. You have stood by me and listened to me. Thank you for being in my corner. You are a blessing in my life. You do so much for others. It doesn't go unnoticed. You are a gem. Don't ever forget that. I love you, my friend.

Regina Rogers, aka "Frienta," aka "Queens" — Thank you for being my friend, mentor, sister in the Lord, support, and more. You are an encourager. You are loving and kind. You have such a meek and gentle spirit. I thank God for you daily, woman of God.

Then there is Brother Mark and Nina Smart-Dixon. Brother Mark has encouraged me about my writings. He and Nina both have been in my corner. He has nicknamed me "Scribe" so much that there are times he doesn't remember my actual name. ☺ It is all good. Thank you both for your love, support, and encouragement during this process that was not easy.

Chris Coker, one of my best friends in the whole world, is always in my corner. She is a cheerleader to say the least. Thank you sis. Love you dearly.

My dearest friend, Elizabeth Herrion, thank you for being a listening ear and for your encouragement, friendship, your love and more. You are one of kind, to say the least.

I now introduce a powerhouse, woman of God in my life, Cynthia Duncan, who is a dear friend, sister in the Lord, and one of my mentors. She is one of the strongest women I know. She is an encourager, she uplifts you, she ministers to you, she is direct, she sugarcoats nothing. I love this about her. She is a jewel, to say the least. She does everything in love. She is non-judgmental, very caring, and giving. She gives of herself and of her time just to be in your presence. What I mean by that is, she is one of support. She is the real deal. Thank you, sis, for having my back.

Then there is my friend and sister Bridget Ouarara. She is an encouragement to me, as well. She has a great listening ear. We take our walks and talk. She is an amazing person to talk with. She is a joy to be around. Bridget has a kind, gentle, and caring soul. She has a lot of wisdom and knowledge to impart.

She loves God and people. She is amazing.

Then there is Brecka Henderson. Now this is my girl right here. She is an encourager to say the least. As you read my book you will know why. She is very essential in my life. She does my hair and other beauty treatments. I thank God for her encouraging words to me. Even, when I was at my heaviest, with my weight, and I didn't like or love myself, she just knew what to say, and she is real about it. She encouraged me like no other. She still does to this day. She is more than a beautician. She is a songbird. She is a worship leader. She loves the Lord. A very giving, uplifting, encouraging of a person that I have ever seen. She is really gifted. She is a strong woman. Thank you, my friend.

Jennifer Smallwood, I thank God for you my friend and prayer warrior. You have been there for me, listened to me, as well as ministered to me when I have needed it. You never once judged me. You are such a beautiful person on the inside and out. Thank you for your heart in listening to the Lord when taking me in inner healing. Thank you so much. The ministry that you have is greatly needed.

Missy Hartman, I just love you. You are one of the sweetest people that I know. You have been in my corner and been there with me for these past few years in inner healing. You have listened while I have broken and cried. It didn't matter the time, and not once did you ever judge me. You stayed with me. You are still with me. I thank God for you.

Dottie Halter, I love you, my friend. Thank you for being in my corner and a part of the inner healing crew. I love your spirit and love for others. How you genuinely care and want to see others set free. Thank you for your guidance, your love, your care, and your gentleness. Also, for your encouragement. It takes a village to raise me. ☺

There are so many people to thank. If I have not mentioned your name, I apologize in advance. There have been so many people in my corner. I thank you all for your love. I don't know where I would be otherwise. Most importantly, I want to thank God for His goodness and grace. Without God it is hard to live and to be. As people, we face many challenges in life. But with God all things are possible according to His Word in Luke 1:37.

Psalms 34:19 (NLT) says, "The righteous person faces many troubles, but the Lord comes to the rescue each time."

Trouble doesn't always last. I am living proof of this. God has brought me up and out of so many things, including myself. God is good.

Everyone that I have mentioned here has played an important role in my life. There are some whom I didn't mention, but there are many more who have stood by me, whom I have not mentioned because I didn't get their permission. I respect their privacy. They have been in my corner and have not bailed out on me. I am one pretty blessed woman. Too, I do not want to forget my children and grandchildren, who have been a support during this time.

INTRODUCTION

I am going to share my journey of how my life came about. It is a testimony to God's grace, mercy, loving kindness that has been extended to me. This book is worth the read. It is a testimony of my life and where God has brought me from.

Today, I want to give honor and praise to the Most-High God, for all that He has done for in my life. He alone has brought me a mighty long way. I was a person who had no self-worth, no self-esteem; I didn't think I was either beautiful or loveable.

Growing up I was called stupid, fat, ugly, among other names. They said, "You won't amount to anything" and "I hate you and wish you were dead." This affected me for many years. Even my marriage was very abusive. My ex-husband would call me out of my name, threaten me, and use intimidation and violence as a way to keep me bound.

From the time I was a child, to teenager, and even in my marriage that was unfixable and with a son I raised on my own without much support, I had not taken care of myself. God has placed me in a position to where I have to face me and take care of myself. I am so grateful and blessed. God is good to me.

God has positioned me where I am currently. That is taking care of me in all areas of my life.

Before I go on, my perceptions of God use to be so skewed, as result of all the abuse and trauma that I have suffered in my childhood and marriage. The things said over me affected me in many ways. The way I was treated led me to think that God was this way, too. At one point, I thought God was a monster. I thought God didn't like me. None of this is truth. The enemy, Satan, tries to deceive us and will use whatever means to do it, whether it is through people or circumstances.

Today, I know God for myself, and He is good. God is an amazing God.

God has brought me to my senses. It has been a long journey toward healing and wholeness.

Only with God's help and love for me have I survived and am now living a victorious life in Him.

Chapter 1-My Childhood

My father was a miner, and my mother was a stay-at-home mom. Well, she was supposed to be. I was the oldest of six children. When we were a little older, at times my mother would get a job. Having an employed mother, when the only thing you want is a mother, makes life a little difficult.

My earliest memories of life begin around age three. We lived with my great-grandfather. There were three of us kids living there. We had ranged from one to three years of age. I recall my parents getting ready to go somewhere, but they were trying to decide which one of us was going to stay with my great-grandfather and which two were going with them. Well, of course, I was the one who had to stay home. I don't know why they weren't taking all three of us, but they didn't. I was so upset and crying. I just didn't understand why I wasn't allowed to go.

There wasn't anything wrong with my great-grandfather. He was cool. I just wanted to go, but I rarely got to go with them. When we lived with my great-grandfather, I thought he was so funny. I loved living with him. He made it fun for us. He would stick out his teeth and I thought that was the neatest thing ever. I tried to do that and wasn't able to. Every time he would stick out his teeth, we would get tickled and start laughing. My great-grandfather would, too. I never knew until I got older it was false teeth, and they could be removed. To this day, the thought of my grandfather doing that still makes me laugh.

We lived with him for a few years. I remember one day my mother put us to bed during the day, because we were in trouble for something. What it was? I don't know. I remember I had to go to the bathroom, and she took a shoe and busted my butt, leaving a bruise. I felt that was totally uncalled for. I was only three years old. Good grief!

Also, while living there with my great-grandfather, he had this huge garden. When I got older, I wanted a garden like his. He had this house and a big fenced-in yard with a peach tree and a bench that surrounded the tree. We would play out in the yard while my great-grandfather sat on that bench with us. He really enjoyed watching us play.

We had a dog that was a collie who was red and white. We named him Big Red. He would always play with us kids. I loved that dog. One day he was under my father's truck and didn't come out. Later, I found out that Big Red had died. I blamed my father for Big Red's death. I felt if Big Red wasn't under the truck he would not have died. My father was in the truck while it was running. It had to be his fault. It wouldn't be the last time that one of our animals would die.

When I was about five, we moved into a one-bedroom house. It was a small house for five people. We were in the same town as my great-grandfather, but across the road. We could walk to my great-grandfather's house and back. I was always glad to see him.

When I was about six years old, my great-grandfather died. I was very upset. Back then I didn't know anything about death. All I knew was he was in the hospital and not coming back. I remember going to the funeral home, seeing him laid out; at the time there was hardly anyone else in the room. I really didn't know much at all, except that he wasn't with us anymore. I truly loved him. He was awesome. There isn't any day that goes by that I don't miss him.

During the time when we lived in this new house that was too small for us, we had a barn out back. My parents had gotten a horse. She was wild. We called her Cocoa. We would ride her. She was funny. Every chance she got, she would escape her barn, run around the house, and run through town. We kids would purposely leave the back door open. She had run around the house and would stick her head in the door. Then she would take off down to town. They would have to go and chase her. She came back and would do it again. Every time, we kids would open the door, she would stick her head in the door. To us it was funny.

One day they sold her due to her biting me. I was so upset about that. If my uncle would have listened to me in the first place, she would not have bitten me. I tried to tell him she would bite me. He told me to continue to hold the rope, and that is when she bit me. They took me to the emergency room, and I had to get two shots. I loved that horse.

After a while, they brought home a puppy and they named him, "Pooh Bear." He was white and very tiny. We didn't have him very long at all. All I was told was that Pooh Bear disappeared. I never knew what happened to him. This wouldn't be the last time that something happened to our pets.

We had two more collies. One was brown and white, and his name was Brownie. The other collie was black and white, and his name was Skunky. My aunts came to get me, my brother, and my sister. Brownie followed us and got hit by a car and was killed. My sister was crying. Then Skunky died not too long after that. He had a rope around his neck and was foaming at the mouth. Skunky had hidden under the house. I remember my mother saying he was choking on a bone. She called the police, and they came and got Skunky. He was gone and we never saw him again.

In 1972, my mother had another little brother, so now there were four kids and two adults in this one-bedroom house. We were there by ourselves most of the time. My mother was gone — God only knows where — and my father was gone, too. I remember my baby brother was on the couch, crying. I was little and didn't know how to take care of him. This was at a time when my mother wasn't at home taking care of us.

In 1974, my mother had another little brother and now there were five kids and two adults living in this one-bedroom house. My mother was still never around and would leave us to fend for ourselves. My father, if he wasn't at work, was at my grandparent's house.

Sometimes I went to stay overnight at my grandmother and grandfather's house. I was eight years old at the time. My aunts and I were outside, and I was smoking a cigarette. My grandmother caught them allowing me to smoke. My grandmother got onto them. She was afraid if my father found out, she would be in trouble. No, I would have been. Today, I hate cigarettes.

At the age of eight, I did go to church off and on. I had been thinking about God since I was five years old. When I was eight, I wanted to give my heart and life to Christ. I wanted to go to the altar but was afraid. I had wished I had gone anyway. I wouldn't be until years later that I did give my heart to Christ.

In 1975, things turned worse for me. This was where shame and guilt had crept in.

This part of my life is very difficult to share without crying. As usual, my parents were not around. At this particular time, I was nine years old. The boy who lived up the street from me came to our house. He took me into the woods behind our house and had his way with me. He did this not only to me, but he also did this to my sister. She was seven years old at the time. When my mother and father found out, my mother took a belt to me and beat me in front of my father. He laughed in my face calling me, "Weedzee." I hate this name to this day. My mother didn't do that to my sister. She called the police and made a report of rape on her. This caused a distance between me and my sister. For years I had hated my sister because of this. Any time my sister would do something, she would never get into trouble, it was always my fault, or I would be blamed for the things she would do.

I felt so ashamed for many years, even into my adulthood because of this. As time went on, things got progressively worse. After this happened, any time my mother would get pissed off, she would call the police on this kid. I don't know why, but she did.

Not only was I shame based, but I felt guilt, too. I didn't know how to handle this at my age.

Another incident that occurred was my brother got mad at me; as usual, my father had gone to my grandparents. And my mother, who knew? My father's BB gun was lying on the bed in the living room, but the safety was off. My brother picked up the gun. I turned my head, and he shot me in my temple. He was angry and had done it on purpose. I screamed and started crying. My father was called, and he came home. I was in the other room looking at my head. I heard him hollering at my brother, and he came in and saw me for a minute. Then he turned around and left to go back to my grandparent's house. I wasn't checked out; all he did was ask if I was okay. He didn't tend to me. He just turned around and left again.

For me that was one of the two worst years of my life. Things didn't end there; it just grew worse.

The plumbing in our house went out. They dug a trench in the yard, but it didn't fix the problem. We had no functioning bathroom. We had to use a pot.

We had the woods, and we kids were made to dump it when it was full, even if it was dark outside. If we didn't, our father would call us worthless and tell us we didn't deserve anything. It would be worse if we didn't empty the pot when we were told to. We didn't have running water in the house, so we had to boil water to take baths. In junior high, I was told I smelled like fish. In other words, I stunk and needed a bath. I was made fun of in school.

I remember going up the stairs in junior high and my pencil accidentally jabbed one of the girls I went to school with. I went to apologize, but she got mad and called me "Trash." Even in high school, she made fun of me. Needless to say, I didn't like her at all. I wasn't trash. No one knew what I had been going through. It didn't matter what I was going through, she had no right to call me that.

Then the incident happened. We kids were outside playing, and these two beagle puppies were walking through our yard. My mother pulls up, and runs them over, like nothing happened. She gets out of the car and goes inside, gets a trash bag and shovel, puts them in a trash bag and what she did with them, I don't know. She showed no emotion, didn't say anything to us or said a word of any kind. I was afraid of her. When I saw this happen, my fear of her only intensified. It didn't faze her. She didn't say anything to us and went on as though nothing had happened. It was all senseless to me.

As I had gotten a little older, when my parents would be gone, my older brother and I would get into it. He used to make me so mad, I would take a can of pop and bust it above his head. There were two times in my life that he had made me so mad. I had put up with him antagonizing me; I punched him in his gut a few times. He has been mean to me and put dog poop in my hair. He has done some stuff. This is the same brother who had shot me in my temple.

I saw him chase my younger brother up a tree. My younger brother was so high up on a limb and had fallen out of the tree and hurt his shoulder. Did my parents take him to the doctor? No. My little brother was maybe four or five years old, if that. He wasn't attended to or taken to the doctor.

There were times my cousin would come over to our house and I remember getting so mad at her. I took a tent pole to her. My mother took it to me. I had lots of anger inside of me. I had no idea how bad it was. I was so jealous of her. I had felt she had taken my place as my mother's daughter.

We had another dog. Her name was "Moon Beam." Where she got her name, I don't know. Anyhow, she had four litters of pups. In each litter, she had ten pups. We kids would pick out our pups. Did they stay alive? No! During this time, I was probably eleven years old. I started staying at my cousin's husband's grandmother, to help her out. They paid me to do this. There were times I would come home, and the pups would be lying out in the yard by the water pump dead, their throats all ripped out. I didn't know what happened to them. I never knew.

When I was away and staying with Mrs. Braden, my mother came to visit. My mother wanted money from me. I was eleven years old, and she was asking for money from me. At home I had a puppy named "Fluffy," who was one of the pups out of the last litter. She went on to say that my brother, Bart, had dropped Fluffy on his neck and had broken his neck. This was my mother's way to try and get money from me. She never made sense. I believe back then that she was probably drinking and using, but it was never in the house. I had this huge feeling that Bart didn't do it. I believe she killed my dog. Also, I believe she used that as a way for me to give her money, even though it didn't make any sense.

My mother had been working at this factory and someone had given her some kittens. We only had those kittens for a week. They began to stagger around and died. Every animal we ever had died. After all of this, I wasn't able to connect to animals, with so much loss. If someone else had a pet, I could pet them, but I didn't want to be close to animals anymore after all of this.

Our mother did get worse. When she would go to the store, she would turn around and scream bloody murder at us. We were kids and we had no idea what we had done. We had just walked in the door. There was no being nice, not with her.

I remember another incident where my sister had gotten a hold of my mother's cigarettes and she had broken them. I took them from her, to put them back in the pack, and who walks in? My mother. I told her what had happened and she screamed at me, calling me a liar. I got into trouble; my sister did not.

Again, my sister got away with it. She was my mother's favorite and couldn't do any wrong. I don't recall her getting into trouble for anything, ever. She was not innocent.

I had taken a lot of physical abuse from my mother. She would slap me across my face, pull my hair, punch me, and was always screaming at me. I was so timid and afraid of her. Look what she did to those puppies when they came in the yard. What would she do to me?

I was a child, what did I do that was so bad? I know that I had not done anything to her, not ever.

When I was twelve years old, we moved into a bigger house, not too far away. We were still in the same school district.

As my sister and I had gotten older, we were constantly fighting. There would be knock-down, drag-outs fights. One day I would get her; the next day she would get me. It was constant. It was sad because we were so divided. We were not close at all.

When I was fourteen, my mother screamed bloody murder at me, hollering, "I hate you and wish you were dead!" I was so hurt, wondering what I had done for her to say this. The rejection of my mother hurt me badly. Not only had I felt rejection, but also abandonment, guilt, increasing amounts of shame, self-hatred, and blame for things I had not even done to her. It didn't matter — she hated me. She was full of false promises. Even in my adulthood. I wanted no part of my mother's life. I didn't trust her. I couldn't. But yet she wanted me to respect her, and I couldn't give her that. I ended up hating her. The pain was rooted deep.

When my mother would work at the college, during ballgames I could work cleaning tables, sweeping, and mopping. I wasn't eighteen yet. It was a way to make me some money. I would get tips and she told me to put them in the tip jar. She said everyone put their tips in there. So, I did, but do you think I saw any of it? No, she took it, plus the money I made. She wouldn't give me my money. I would have two dollars and she would want it. She would scream at me to get it.

There was a turnaround for me. In 1979, it was summer, my mother sent me to church camp. At the time I was mad. I was the only one she sent. I ended up giving my heart over to God then. For the first time ever, I had felt peace in my life. It was the best feeling. It didn't last, because I was living in Hell and didn't know how to live a life of a Christian. I have gone to church off and on. My father would go to church off and on. He was a Sunday school teacher, Royal Ranger Leader, and the Superintendent of the Church. He would come home and was mentally and emotionally abusive to his children.

He would tell me how fat and ugly I was and laugh in my face. He would say to us, "you want respect, you got to earn it." Also, he would say, "I am always right, and you are always wrong."

We didn't have to do anything to get in trouble. When it came to him, you stayed in trouble. You didn't have to do anything. He was never satisfied.

Not only this, but my oldest brother also wouldn't leave me alone. I told my father. What happened next, I never saw coming. He smacked my brother across the kitchen chairs. I couldn't believe it.

There was another incident. It was winter and it had snowed. We had a wood stove; my father took the tray of ashes from the stove and looked like he was going to throw it out in the snow. He didn't.

He got mad at my oldest brother and threw the ashes on him. I couldn't believe he had thrown the ashes on him. We could never do right in his sight. He always posed as this good man. I am sorry to say, no he wasn't.

I was an emotional mess. I had just started going to high school, and the principal pulled me aside and asked me if I would like to go back to middle school again. I told him, "No, I want to move on with my life."

In 1981, my youngest brother was born. Now there were six kids brought into this mess.

Things progressed even worse. My mother still wasn't there most of the time.

If she was, you never knew what type of mood she would be in. When I had come home one day, the lights were out, and she was sitting in a chair in the corner, with her knees to her chest, a cigarette in her hand, her eyes closed and in another world. I left her alone.

Then when she was angry, if I wasn't getting the blunt of her rage, my brother Jaden was. I was at a friend's house out on the porch, and she pulled up and beat him with a switch in front of his friends as hard she could, gets back into the car, and left. She was crazy to say the least.

Instead of being at home, cleaning the house, she was who knows where. Our house was filthy, there were maggots all over the kitchen sink, trash, and even on our kitchen table, because she would not clean. I would have to take a bottle of bleach and clean the table off with it before I could get anything else done. I hated living like this. I vowed my house would never be like this and it isn't. I can't stand this kind of stuff. It drives me crazy.

When she was home, she was either passed out on the couch or in one of her fabulous moods. I dreaded that.

One day I came home for lunch, to let her know my brother had taken my money. I had a friend with me; my mother was passed out on the couch. When I ask her, she screamed bloody murder at me, in front of her. We left. I was humiliated and embarrassed. Why couldn't I have a decent mother?

One afternoon, I came home, and she demanded I clean the house. I told her I had homework. She said to me, "I will tell your dad!" I was so pissed. She was a stay-at-home mother, supposed to take care of the home. I wondered why she didn't ask my sister or brothers to help. Oh no! The princess never had to do anything.

There was an incident when my mother was home. She and I had gotten into a fight. My sister was there. My mother kicked me out of the house. My father was where he usually was, when he wasn't working, at my grandparents. I walked across town to my aunt and uncles and borrowed their phone. I called him and told him what had happened. He came home to investigate; my mother denied it.

My mother's behavior had gotten worse. At the time, I didn't know what was wrong with her. I recall Christmas of 1981 or 1982. It came Christmas, we had no presents. My father said he worked all the overtime he could for so we would have a good Christmas. I remember that year; my grandmother had given me a ring and money. I was grateful for that. As kids, we were devastated. I don't think my mother was even there. It seemed like all she did was take from us. She got to the point that she would not cook or bring food into the house. She would bring my father food from the restaurant, but for us it was most of the time bread or occasionally chicken. I didn't know what was going on then.

She supposedly went to the laundromat when she brought our clothes back they were folded and dirty. She was getting worse.

My mother and father didn't believe us when we were sick. I had been sick for two weeks. I was in pain. My father asked my mother, "Do you think she is faking?" I went to the doctor, and I had a kidney infection. I had a follow-up appointment; my mother dropped me off and took off. I went inside, but I didn't stay for the appointment. I was sitting outside the doctor's office, waiting for her to return. I sat on those steps for at least two hours. I was wondering if she was going to come back.

She did, I didn't ask her where she had been. She didn't ask about the doctor visit either. We just went home.

In 1981, a friend and former teacher of mine invited me to church. I went to a revival one night and rededicated my life to Christ. The peace I felt once before came back. I started going to church and I stayed a while this time. I eventually went back to the one I grew up in.

Right before my mother left, my sister and I got into a horrible fight. The worst we had ever been in. It was the scariest fight she and I ever got into. We were throwing my brother's rocking chair and broke it. My brother Jaden brought in a butcher knife, and I took it, I was going to stab her. I had it with her. Thank God Jaden took the knife. I never wanted to do that kind of thing to my sister, ever. It was my mother's fault, not my sister's.

My mother had done a number on me. Why she would cause division between her own kids is beyond me. She was not a well woman.

When I was about16, my brother Clyde and I went to the doctor. I had broken out with blood blisters all over my back and face. They were painful and stuck to my clothes. My doctor put me on Accutane. I was on this medicine for six months. I was not allowed out in the sun. It had made my skin crack and bleed. I had to continue to see my doctor.

My mother was supposed to have been working evenings. She should have been home by 10 P.M. and wasn't. I waited up for her. She didn't get home until maybe 20 minutes before my father had gotten home from work. She was acting strange, talking about some man. It was 4 A.M. and I had to be at school at 8 A.M. I was worried about her.

After that she had taken off for a few days. We didn't know where she was. I was at school, and she called me there. I went home and told my father. He then made her leave. I thought finally "she is gone." She made my life Hell. When she left, she took my baby brother, my sister, and my oldest brother. It was me and two of my younger brothers.

I had taken on her responsibilities that she had not been doing anyway. I had to clean the house, take care of my brothers, and go to school. I had resentment toward my parents. My brothers were not the problem. It was both my father and mother. I thought since she left, it would be better, but it wasn't.

I got to the point that I wouldn't eat. I was so stressed out. I was a wreck. Living with my father was not easy. When this all started, I was relieved, because I didn't have to wonder about her.

My father was a miner. One week he would work days and another week he would work evenings. This particular week, he had to work evenings. He knew my mother was coming, so we had to stay with my aunt and uncle. My mother came and crawled through the window and took my clothes. It was all right. I finally got some new ones.

My father told me that I wasn't allowed to leave and go anywhere. When he got off work, he would take my baby brother and go to my grandparents. I was still expected to watch my other two brothers.

They weren't my responsibility — they were his. My father suddenly started going back to church. It was because he wanted a good character reference from the pastor. My father played a good game. He would run through the house praising Jesus. Then next, he would be screaming "You're fat and ugly," and laughing in my face again. Nothing I did was right.

My nerves were worse than they ever were. I kept going to church, doing my best to hang on. The person I went to church with was my neighbor. She would come, pick me up and take me. I never wanted to ride with my father. I felt more comfortable with her.

Also, I wasn't allowed to see my grandmother. I was hurt about that. When he would drop me off to do laundry, I would go to the pay phone and call her. My brother told on me, so I would sneak around and call her. He never knew.

My father put me through the ringer. Not only this, but my sister had left. My father was mad at her for that. I didn't blame my sister for leaving. My father called her a whore. She was only 14 and was not a whore.

I was so mad.

Also, my older brother would send my father letters. We would go to my aunt and uncle's place, and he would read those letters out loud. My brother told my father in the letters he loved him. What came next, I didn't expect. They were all laughing. It was highly inappropriate. What both my parents had done and caused ruined our family dynamics. We were eight broken people, who went separate ways, with a ton of hurt and pain.

My father said at the time that my mother had been drinking. I didn't believe him. I had to find out for myself. They were going through a divorce, and it was bitter with six children stuck in the middle of the madness, whether we were together or not.

Our home life was chaotic, to say the least.

My friend, Anna, told my father that my mother had a boyfriend and was taking my father's paychecks to her boyfriend. My father almost lost the house because of my mother. My sister knew about this, because she was with her, and so was my friend Anna.

My father had grilled Anna and he didn't have a right to do that. Not only this, Anna's father just had a heart attack. My father was relentless. He had her subpoenaed to court.

She was under 18. I told her she didn't have to do that. My father got mad at me and told me to shut up. I was mad. It was all about him and his ego.

My father obtained an attorney. My mother had, as well. The battle begins. They were both ruthless. I found out she hired my teacher's husband. Oh, fabulous. The incident that occurred nine years earlier, when the boy up the street had his way with me and my sister, my mother brought that up in court too. The family was there and I was talking to them. I felt bad for them. Why drag them into this? It had nothing to do with them. That was done and over with. I certainly didn't want to be reminded. My mother loved keeping the situation going. She was straight up crazy.

The first time we went to court, it was to determine custody of six children. I had to go testify against my own mother. My father thought I would lie for on his behalf. Guess what? No, I wasn't. I was on the side of right. Neither one of my parents was on the side of right. My father told me he would get me a car for graduation and brothers' bikes. He lied. One of the things I was asked was if my father promised me a car and my brothers a bike. I told them he did. He was mad and the lawyer wasn't happy either. I wasn't going to lie about it.

I asked the courts if I could go to my grandma's to stay overnight. The courts granted it. My father made sure he was there bright and early Saturday morning. All I did was get into the car. He said, "You can't go back, you have changed." I only stayed one night, and I just got into the car. Again, I was mad. He never ceased his controlling ways. I still snuck around and called my grandmother. There was no way he could keep me from her.

I had gone to my doctor, and he asked me what was going on at home. I told him my parents were getting a divorce. This was how bad things were affecting me.

I had it with my father for the longest time. I was packing my clothes and leaving. My youngest brother, who was three at the time, started crying and saying, "Beth, don't leave me." I started crying and put everything back. I couldn't leave. I couldn't leave him.

Christmas of 1983 came and I decided to go to my aunt and uncle's for Christmas. My father said my mother was an alcoholic. I wanted to find out for myself. I go there to find out it was the truth. I was devastated. She hid it as far as not having any in the home. I get home and my father was upset with me for going. He said, "You had a choice, but the boys didn't. I am disappointed in you, the lawyer is disappointed in you, and the family is disappointed you." You know what, it was nothing new. My father was always disappointed in me.

It caused me to sink into a deep depression as a result of his high expectations. I went to the counselor at school to ask for help. She didn't want to get involved, but she did. I started going to counseling. My father didn't like that at all. I didn't care. One day, he came into the kitchen; he was going on about it. He said, "I don't understand why you have to go to counseling and can't talk to me?" It hit his ego hard. I got mad and threw an empty can and hit him upside his head. He got mad and started yelling at me. I took off into my bedroom and he followed me as he continued to yell at me.

Not only this, my grandmother had written me a letter and I was waiting for it. I never received it. One night we were on our way home from the grocery shopping. My aunt Melissa was with us. My father said, "Oh, by the way your grandma sent you a letter. I opened it and read it." Then he went on to say what she had written. In the letter, my grandmother was saying how both my father and mother were being selfish. It hurt his ego that the truth was spoken. He went on to say, "I burnt it." He was laughing about it. I was so mad. He put me through some stuff.

My counselor had me and my father come to a session together. I was mad and hollering about my father reading my mail and burning it. The counselor got onto me for disrespecting my father. I was mad. I was always mad. I felt that he didn't deserve any respect.

It got to the point it was so bad I had thoughts of suicide three different times, I had a razor, ready to cut my wrist. Each time, my friend Anna came to see about me. I would quickly hide it behind my back. She asked how I was. She never knew what I had behind my back and that I was suicidal. After she left, I would put it away, and eventually I never thought about that again.

I had a diary, and my father had gotten a hold of it and read that, too. I had no privacy, was not allowed to be teen, and I couldn't go anywhere. I felt like I was his prisoner. That is why I left. He was mad at me; from that point on, I was the black sheep of the family. He disowned me; I was not there to be controlled. I wasn't his slave.

It wasn't just all of this. Also, a woman came to our house and just walked in the door. My father, one of my uncles, and we kids were there. She said that we had an older brother; and he was only a few months older than I. My father laughed and denied it.

Not only this, apparently, I have two more brothers I have not met, but I have known about them for years. My sister had told me that one of the boys came to my father's door and said he was his son. Par for the course, my father did what he did best and rejected him. I have wanted to search for my three brothers for years. I just don't know how to do that. Hopefully one day I will be able to.

My father has issues with women. He always has and always will and thinks he is funny to shun women. He doesn't talk to women right.

I called my grandmother and told her. This was the straw that broke the camel's back. I was done. I turned 18 on the 9th of April and the divorce was the 13th. We had to go to court. We older ones got to go into the judge's chambers. Since I was the oldest, I went first, I told the judge I wanted to go to my grandma's and live. I didn't want either of my parents. The judge asked if I had anything else I wanted to say. I said no. My mother drove me to my grandmother's. I had two months left of school and I wanted to finish. The school I attended, previously, I had gone to my whole life. I had two months to finish. I went to a different school.

I finished school and graduated by the skin of my teeth.

While living with my grandmother, my uncle was an instigator. He loved drama. He got me and my grandmother into an argument. I had had it. I went into his medicine cabinet and took out some pills. Before I had taken them, I prayed to God and said to Him, "I don't want to die; I just don't want to hurt anymore." I put half of the pills back and took the rest. I was out for a day and a half. When I had woken up, there was my grandmother wiping my face off with a cold rag.

My grandmother had called Doug, who was with the Division of Family Services (DFS) and told him about what had happened. Doug was already involved with our family before I moved out of my father's house. Also, he was someone my grandmother and uncle knew. He had come by to see me, but I was already out with my friend.

In June of 1984 I had graduated high school. In June, my grandmother said I couldn't stay with her anymore and I was being sent to live with my aunt and uncle, whom I did not want to live with. My mother (the drunk) and sister were already living there. I dreaded going there. While living there, it wasn't easy. My mother didn't like me at all. Anything I felt that I should have gotten to do, like drive the car, she allowed my cousin to do. She doted over my sister and my cousin. I felt like she put my cousin in my place as her daughter. I was jealous of her and at one point I didn't like her, either. Today, I realized all that had happened was not her fault. Back then, I didn't know any better. I was emotionally messed up. My mother kept going out and getting drunk with her friends. My mother wasn't very nice at all.

One day, my aunt, my uncle, one of my uncle's sons from a previous marriage, and my mother were standing on one side of the table, with me on the other side, standing. They told me I needed to respect my mother. I said I didn't have to. The respect didn't mean anything to me. When it came to my mother, I had no respect for her. She was abusive and out of control and no one did anything to help us kids.

One incident that happened while living there was my cousin, sister, and I shared a room. I slept on the floor. My uncle came into the room and tried to get on top of me. I told him to get off me. He said, "SHHH."

He tried to do that twice. Then I didn't tell anyone. I lived in fear that if I did, my mother would do to me, what she had done to me when I was nine years old. That was about ten years previously. I wasn't risking that. Later, as an adult, I did tell my mother. She actually believed me, probably because it was done to my sister. I wasn't face to face with her. It was by phone. She wasn't even mean about it. I was in shock.

While living there, I did get a babysitting job. One night, my sister, my cousin, and I went to get some liquor. I paid for it; I gave the money to one of my cousins to get the alcohol. My sister and I split a six pack, and my cousin drank whiskey or something. I was not a drinker. Three beers made me tipsy. I walked into a convenience store to see if they had a bathroom and they said no. We went to a gas station and the bathroom was dark, the lid on the stool was raised and I fell in. We got home. I was hollering loudly. My cousin said, "Shh you're going to wake them up!" I didn't care.

Eventually after a while, I couldn't stand it there anymore and left. When I was leaving, I was out on the porch waiting for my ride, and my uncle was standing on the porch with his hands in his pockets. He said to me, "You know you can't come back." I said to him, "I know." I didn't care either, because I never wanted to live there in the first place. I had to leave and get away from there. I was staying with one of my mother's friends. She was really nice. I was still babysitting. I was going to help them out for allowing me to stay there. She had teen kids. I went to move with my mother's friend. Well guess who paid me a visit? My mother. She wanted money from me. It didn't matter whether I had any money or not. I told her no. I didn't have any. She started screaming at me, "You liar!" I ended up caving in, because I didn't want to get into it with my raging mother. By this time, I was 19 years old. She was vicious; I hated her all the more.

My mother and her friends were always drunk. One night, one of her friends wanted me to drive. I didn't have my driver's license then. I may have told them. I don't know. Delana and her boyfriend were so drunk. They handed me the keys. The wrong thing to do was give me the keys. I had forewarned them. Tabitha was with us. Delana and her boyfriend sat in the back. I wasn't a good driver then. Thank God a police officer didn't pull us over. I would have been in so much trouble. I guess that was the highlight of my pain.

My mother and a group of her friends would meet in a restaurant. I asked her for a soda. Again, she would scream at me and yell at me, "No!" She had been sitting there eating and drinking her stuff. She was cruel.

Another incident, she was drunk, and she picked up pots and pans and was going to hit me with them. Her friend Delana grabbed them and told me I needed to respect her. I didn't have to do or say anything for my mother to hit me. All I did was stand up, because she was ready to hit me. I wasn't going to take it anymore.

My mother's friend Vicky whom I had been living with, had a boyfriend with three kids; she had two and me. We all moved in with them.

It was ok for a while. They weren't bad people. It was just too many people in one place.

The incident I recall was when my mother came over and she was hugging on Vicky's boyfriend's daughter. I was fine with that. I went over to give her a hug and she pushed me and screamed at me to get away from her. I was upset. I couldn't understand what her problem was. I never knew. I sometimes wondered if I was really hers. She treated me like crap. Eventually, I went to live with a family who pastored a church I grew up in. I had not been in church in probably a good year. I went back to church, gave my heart back to Christ. They had given me my own room, and for the first time in my life, I felt real peace. I was in a stable home. My aunt gave me a job, I went to church, I got back into counseling, and I was thriving. I spent hours in the Word, reading, and praying. Even so, I still had severe trauma issues. Back then, I had no idea of that. I went to see my counselor's husband to be put on medication. I told him no. I had faith to believe I would recover. He thought differently. I didn't allow him to sway my decision.

Then, after two months of living with them, I moved three and half hours away.

I have lived where I am now since 1985, all except when I moved out of state with my now ex-husband for one and half years.

My grandmother had been sick. She went into the hospital twice per year. She always came home. I had sent her a letter while she was in the hospital and when she knew I was going to be fine where I was, she died. I cried my eyes out. She was the closest thing to a mother I had; her own daughter had been really cruel to me. I never told my grandmother. My grandmother had always defended me, too. It didn't matter the way my uncle was. She and I were very close.

There are times I miss her so much. Just the thought of her knowing I would be fine helped me through all these years. To me, this is a God thing.

Was I still a mess? Definitely, I was and would be for a long time. God kept working on me, day after day, month after month, and year after year. He is still working on me.

For four years, I was free of being abused. I lived nearly 200 miles away from my hometown. I always thought of my siblings. The sibling I thought about the most was Jaden. I thought about him often. Around holidays, I was very lonely. I would think about my brother often. He started drinking at age ten and started using drugs later on. While living with our father, I did tell him, and he did nothing. My brother struggled with addiction for 31 years. He eventually died. From 2010 until he died in 2013, he was in and out of the hospital at least 24 times. Always near death. Three weeks before his death, Easter had come early that year. I had prayed for him and asked God not to let him leave this earth without him making it right with Him. My brother didn't think he was worthwhile and he had no self-esteem either. One day. I said to him before he died, "You are worthwhile." He said to me, "You believe that?" I said, "Yes."

On Easter Sunday, he had gone to a church where the pastor understood addiction. God knows what He is doing. They had an Easter program, and my brother went forward and gave his heart to Christ. When I heard this, I began to cry. Then three weeks later, he died. My son and his wife were expecting their third child. I told my son that my brother had to die, so my granddaughter could be born. He was buried on that Saturday, and she was born that same day in the afternoon. I didn't go to the funeral. I couldn't, due to family drama.

My sanity depended on me not going. That day was bittersweet day, to say the least.

All in one day, we had a birthday we were celebrating, my brother was being buried, and my granddaughter was being born. I had to stay close to home due to my daughter-in-law getting ready to deliver my granddaughter.

The day of the funeral, I had gone to my son's house where they were holding the birthday party for one of the kids. My daughter-in-law was in labor, so they went to the hospital while we finished the birthday party. Then we went to the hospital where we waited for my granddaughter to arrive, as my brother was being buried. It was a rough day, to say the least. My brother's death hit me hard. I was so mad at my father for my brother's death, even though death is inevitable, and God is no respecter of persons. I felt like if he would have listened to me long ago, my brother would probably still be here with us. How I am to truly know this? My heart was broken. He had a lot to offer, but he honestly didn't get that opportunity.

All I know is my brother's life wasn't good on Earth, but today, seven years later, I know that he is at peace with God.

Chapter 2 - MY MARRIAGE

As I share this part of my life, it is embarrassing, to say the least. Sometimes we get into these relationships thinking they are good for us when in all actuality they are not. This is actually what I had thought. As I continue to share this part of my life, it isn't just written for the sake of writing. I am writing as the Lord leads. As I am

Baring my soul, for not one moment do I take what I am saying for granted. As you will read, I give God the glory for bringing me out of this relationship with my life. I don't know why I allowed this relationship to go on. I know that I am not the only one who has ever done this. I am hoping as you read this and if you are in a domestic violence situation that this will encourage you to have the strength to leave. I am here to shed light on violence in the home and the church. I am making it very clear I am not going against God. I am sharing my life and what my son and I both endured.

Through this time in my life, which covers a ten-year span, I know God as my and my son's protector.

I was 22 years old when I met my now ex –husband. We had dated for eight months and then got married. Let me share with you what had happened.

We met at work; at first, I didn't like him. I thought he was pompous.

One day he asked me out. I told him that I didn't know. Against my better judgment, for whatever reason, I gave him a chance. I should have just kept on walking.

On the first date, he took me out to dinner at a Chinese restaurant, and it was nice. I am like, "Ok, this was good." We did continue to date. I learned he was attending school to become a pastoral counselor. My dream since the age of 12 years old was to be a pastor's wife. We did continue to date.

During the eight months that we dated, many things were going on.

There were issues, but I thought things would get better. I was wrong.

I will be sharing some incidents, but not all of them.

While we were dating, we had stopped by work so I could take my boss something. My boss asked me if I could work right then. I ended up making extra money. I went and told my boyfriend they needed me to stay. He didn't like that. I went on my way, and he went his.

We both worked at the same place and in the same department. Many times, he would get mad and usually for no reason at all. He was known for kicking pots, pans, and industrial-size mixing bowls across the kitchen floor. He never once had gotten in trouble for that. I never understood that. Sometimes coworkers would tease him and he would really get mad.

I recall one night I was left in charge, and we were short staffed. I had asked him to clear the dining room because we had to have dishes washed. He kept ignoring me. He knew the boss left me in charge that night, and he knew he needed to clear that dining room. He just didn't like anyone saying anything to him. One of my guy friends — one that we went to church with, mind you — asked him if I was his Queen Bee. My coworker who had said it and I looked at one another and just started laughing. Leonard didn't like that at all. So he choked our coworker until he was red in his face. I couldn't get him to stop. I was screaming at him, and he wouldn't release our friend. Finally, he did. I asked my other coworker why Leonard would do that. He said it was a guy thing. I am like "guy thing?!" I was floored. You just don't put your hands on people. It was just a joke. I was so mad. He had to meet with our boss the next day. Yet he got away with it again. I didn't understand that.

I was pretty mad. You would think it was all I would take. No, not me. I am one who keeps giving chances that I should have never given. I honestly don't know what I was thinking.

Did I deserve this? Absolutely not! Neither did anyone else.

As we continued to date, one time we had gone out to dinner with friends. I thought we were on a date that night, so you know I thought he was paying for me. Well, once again, I thought wrong. I didn't have any money. He ordered and so did my friends. I didn't order. He kept on eating and my friends and the waitress asked me if I was hungry. I just said no. He kept on eating. Do you think this would cause me to say, "bye"? No. I don't have any answers for this.

Every time I would give him chance after chance. Oh, as I continue you will really think, "she was a glutton for punishment." Did I deserve this treatment? No.

One night I fell at work and hurt my ankle. I went to the ER; my friend Bill took me. I had fractured my ankle and the doctor put an air cast on. Leonard was supposed to give me a ride to work. Wow! Normally I rode the city bus to work. He was going to give me a ride. He waited until it was too late for me to get on a bus and get to work in time. I ended up having to walk to work with my ankle in an air cast. It took me 45 minutes to walk it. Oh, and Leonard walked with me. I was mad to say the least. I didn't say anything. I just went onto work and bore the pain.

When he and I had got engaged, we went to see my adoptive parents. He was trying to call his mother long distance. I don't know what the issue was, but he had one. My cousin and I were sitting at the kitchen table and joking around and laughing as we always did. He got mad at me and chased me into their bathroom and had me up against the wall, threatening me, and said, "You better not do that again." All I was doing was joking with my cousin.

Leonard would say to me out of the clear blue, with no reason to say it, that there was a spot on my neck that a person can touch a certain pressure point and squeeze and make that person unconscious. It freaked me out. Again, don't ask me why I didn't run.

Leonard was in school and went to his class, and said something's about us. He picked me and my friend Saul up. Leonard proceeded to tell me that he had gone to his school and told stuff to his class regarding us. He never did say what. I was really upset and went to the pay phone and called my friend Belinda. So it happens that my best friend Belinda's husband was in that class. I don't know what Leonard went and told his class, whatever, or what he had told them. I do know that my friend's husband had known whatever it was before I did, they didn't talk to me about it. I still to this day don't even know what was said. I called my best friend and told her. She already knew. I was in tears and my friend's husband went to our pastor and told him whatever was said. They didn't even come to me. My friend Belinda had told her husband not to go to our pastor, but he did anyway. When I was on the phone with her, she was upset with him. He apologized to me. Leonard never cared what he said or who he would say it to. My former pastor never even talked to me about it. He assumed things about me that were not true. I was made out to look horrible.

This didn't stop me, either. I married him anyway. I had people in my life that sat me down and said, "I don't want you to marry him, because he will hurt you." Nothing fazed me. I went into a relationship with this person who hated me and despised me. I went for the wrong reasons. I thought I could change him. No one but God can change a person. We can't even change ourselves without God.

I found out as time went on how messed up not only Leonard was, but how messed up I was for allowing this person in, who meant me no good.

In my mind, I thought I couldn't get anyone else. My thinking was jacked up. It was a mess. I wasn't healed in regard to relationships.

In my first year of marriage when we started out, I thought things would change. One morning our car would not start. Leonard went outside to start the car and when it wouldn't start, he punched the windshield and busted it. He then came in and threw himself on the floor and broke his brand-new glasses. I called our pastor, and he came over. He was not happy with Leonard's behavior and did speak to him about it.

Then when work would call at 4:30 A.M. asking if I could come in, Leonard answered the phone and screamed in it and said, "No!" he didn't ask me if I wanted to go. He had to be in control. He was always angry and usually over nothing.

Leonard would come home and tell me about the young girls at work he was lusting over. I was mad. I left for a few days. When I got home, he said to me, "I thought you would forgive me?" I should have stayed gone. I was heated.

I went back and gave him another chance.

Then one of my brothers came to live with us. Leonard would always start fights with him. I had to pull my brother away from Leonard and tell him to leave him alone. Leonard was a mean-spirited person. There are many witnesses to this.

Eventually, I had to tell my brother to leave. It was actually for my brother's own safety.

One time we were driving down the road. We weren't even married I don't even think six months. It was a sunny day outside. I wasn't saying anything; I was just enjoying the ride. Out of the clear blue, Leonard looked at me and said, "If you ever leave me, I will have you declared unfit. Have you committed." I just looked at him. I didn't say anything. Did I keep that in the back of mind? You bet I did.

Also, in June of that year, we went to see his sister. We were playing a board game with his sister and brother-in-law. Leonard got mad because he was losing and kicked the board game and walked out the door. I just shook my head.

The next incident that happened was when my friend was staying with us and needing a ride to work. She and I were asleep. She was in the living room, and I was in my room. Leonard had the light on. All of a sudden, he took a pillow while I was sleeping and hit me upside my head. He called us both jerks. We were sleeping. Italia came in to check on me. He went outside at 4:30 A.M. I asked him what was wrong with him. I don't even recall. This wasn't the only time he would wake me up in the wee hours of the morning.

Leonard was still going to school and still in church.

By this time, we had left our first church together, because I felt it was time to go to another church. I had a dream about it and ask Leonard to check it out.

He did. At that time, I had a funeral to attend. When I got back, I had been there for a long time.

Leonard was able to have a friend whom he told stuff to about me. He went around telling people I was crazy. Wow.

When I got pregnant things had got worse. Bill and Tressa were in the living room. Leonard and I were in the kitchen. I was four months along. I was sitting at the kitchen table. Leonard had gotten mad and flipped the table on my stomach. I didn't tell a soul that he had done that. Not anyone. I thank God every day that He got me out in time.

I was in the beginning of my third trimester and was at work when my water broke. I didn't know what it was. I went home and took a shower and went back to work to finish up my job. I called the city clinic. They wanted me to come in. I said the wrong thing. I was scared. I went to the labor and delivery. I was hooked up to a monitor to watch the baby. The next night my friend Taylor, her husband, and son were coming to see me. Next thing I knew, one nurse was jumping on my bed and another one wheeling me out into the operating room for me to have an emergency C-section. All I knew was that they had put a mask on me, and I was out. Taylor had to call her sister to get a hold of Leonard, who wasn't there. I was really sick. I was in the hospital nine days. My son was in the hospital even longer. I named him "Dillon." He was in the neonatal intensive care unit (NICU) for a long time.

I wasn't treated very well by a few of the staff, but there were a few who did care. I was scared to death. Leonard maybe had come to the hospital three times out of the nine days. Then I had to sit at home alone. On Sundays, he would call me and ask if it were ok for him to go out with his buddy and eat lunch. What could I say? I sat at home alone. Leonard never called to see about me. He didn't offer to bring me anything home, either. Also, Rhoda — who was supposed to be my friend — was being awfully chummy with Leonard right in front of me. If I could have moved, she would have gotten it. He was just as guilty. Eventually she left town and needed to.

Here I was, concerned about my baby. Dillon had been in the NICU for a month. The doctor didn't expect him to live. I had to pretty much deal with this on my own. Dillon weighed three pounds and twelve ounces at birth. It was touch and go. After a month, he got to come home at four pounds and seven ounces. Leonard's mother came to visit. While she was there, Leonard got mad at her and told her to shut up and left. He was so angry at her. She didn't say anything to warrant it. Leonard would get mad at the drop of a hat. I was glad at this time she was there because she was changing Dillon's diaper found a bulge on his groin. We took him to the ER. Thankfully, there was a doctor there who had a daughter my son's age. He took pity on us and sent us to the South Side hospital. They brought in the anesthesiologist to talk with me. They had to do surgery on Dillon. He was back in the hospital. He was there for a few days. That first year he went to doctors a lot. They at one point thought he had water on the brain, and they thought he would have to have a shunt. I praise God that he did not. I cried so much. When we had to take him to a doctor and he saw a white uniform, Dillon would scream bloody murder. He didn't want anything to do with doctors and nurses. He had spent his first month in the NICU being poked and prodded with IVs and a feeding tube up his little nose.

But by the grace of God, he has made it. Glory to God in the highest! Praise God! I can't thank God enough for my son's recovery.

Once Dillon was home, a nurse would come in and weigh him. He kept gaining weight and growing. He was somewhat behind, but eventually surpassed all of the obstacles he faced.

There were many incidents even after Dillon had come home. Everywhere we lived, Leonard would put holes in walls and didn't care. He would turn me over on furniture, when Dillon and I were sleeping; it was always at 3 A.M. He was up with the lights turned on, hollering, punching holes in the wall, and turning over furniture. He even yelled at me, waking me up, saying, "You said you would be here anytime I needed you!"

One time, we were on our way home and Leonard stopped in the middle of the road. He told me to get out and walk home. I was looking in the back seat at Dillon. I said, "No!" I wasn't about to leave my baby in the car with him. Also, I was a few miles from home. He did this out of the blue.

He wrote me a letter and in it he said that it was either my job or him. He would get mad and say that I wouldn't let him be the man of the house. He wanted me to choose between him and the church. I said, "I knew God before you. I chose the church." Leonard got mad and went into the kitchen to get a knife. He lay on the kitchen floor, put the knife in his armpit, and acted crazy. I was in such disbelief. He locked me and my son out of the house. I had to go to my pastor's house. Finally, he let us back in the house.

Then we ended up getting a better place to live. The old landlord came to the new place and asked me what happened with the holes in the wall. I said, "Leonard did that." The old landlord said, "Leonard told me that you did that." I was mad. Leonard lied again. Things still were not better.

No matter what I did, I could never do right. During this time when we lived in our new place, Leonard only intensified. He escalated all the more. One morning he was eating cereal, and I was talking to him. He got mad at me, threw the cereal, and hit me upside my head. It bounced off and hit the wall. He told me I had better have it cleaned up by the time he got back from work. I got a hold of a friend and showed it to her.

I was going up the stairs and he passed me, threatening me that he was going to go get a knife. I ran upstairs to where my son was and locked the bedroom door. Leonard had broken the door frame.

On many occasions, Dillon knew when things were about to happen. He would hide behind furniture and in closets. Lord, how could I allow this?

Eventually, I started seeing a therapist for help. I decided to enroll in college. Leonard didn't like it. I even started working part time. I told Leonard he needed to pay the bills and I would cover me and Dillon. I even asked Leonard to go to couples counseling and at first, he wouldn't go. Things still were not better. I came home one evening and asked

Leonard to put an entertainment center together. He got mad. Dillon was in my lap and ran and hid in the closet. Leonard had a screwdriver in his hand and aimed it at my head. I was too scared to move. Eventually, when Dillon felt safe, he came out and sat on my lap. Leonard didn't care and slapped me. He threatened me that if I didn't go to counseling with him he was going to tell them I chased him around the house with a knife. I told him I would go but I would be telling them everything. But when he did, he tried controlling the session. They had to remove him. I was sitting in the corner, shut down and crying. He ended up going to the psych ward for about nine days. During this time, I had gotten an ex-parte for him not to return home where one partner states that the other partner is dangerous. Whoever the lady proclaimed she was at the hospital said to me, and she was scolding me, "I thought you wanted to work your marriage out?" The moment I take a stand, I meet opposition. He had been crazy and when I took a stand I got scolded. She tried to make me feel bad. I tried to get him to go out of state where he belonged. It didn't work. Also, I called the hospital to inform them that I filed for an *ex-parte* against him, and he needed to be served. I was told it would not be served unless I met him face to face to tell him. I contacted a friend of mine. She went with me. They acted like they didn't know what I was talking about when I get there. My friend and a nurse were in there when I had to do this. I was scared to death. Once my friend and I walked out of the room we could hear him kicking the bed. He was throwing a fit.

When we went to court, another one of my friends went with me. Here came Leonard who sat beside me trying to talk to me. An advocate had to stand between us. What opened my eyes was that Leonard was able to get another car and an apartment. This opened my eyes. I would not have been able to do this.

During our time apart, I get a call from some guy on Thanksgiving Day. How he got our phone number I have no clue. But I believe I know now who he was. I didn't then. He called to say that Leonard was having an affair with his wife. If I needed to talk, I could call him. That was the weirdest call ever. Even the maintenance man asked if I had a boyfriend. I said, "NO!" I told the maintenance guy that Leonard had busted the door frame. The maintenance guy was fine with it. I was being accused again.

Even after all of this, I eventually took him back. Don't ask what I was thinking. I wasn't thinking.

Eventually, after Christmas, he moved back home. I had gone to a convention with a few of my church friends and came back home, only to be told by Leonard, "you have not changed." All I did was come home. Eventually, he talked me into moving out of state. He was surprised and so was I. I thought it might make things better for him. I wanted my marriage to work. Things got better,.0 but not for Dillon and me.

Things didn't stop there. This was before we moved. He got to the point he would terrorize us in the car on Sunday mornings, on our way to church. He would speed down the road and slam on the brakes and I would hit the dashboard. He said we were not going to church. He called me "Ms. Perfect," saying that I never did anything wrong.

This happened to me more than once. He always acted this way, with our son in the car. He had even locked me out of the car. Kept going back and forth until my son screamed for him to stop and let me in. Eventually, Leonard allowed me in the car.

We eventually made it to church, but I was an emotional mess.

At one point, we were going to separate churches. He wanted me to do counseling with his pastor. I get there and Leonard was not there. I was so mad. That pastor told me that I was the one who needed to change. He didn't know anything about me. I get up and walk out. The pastor commanded me to come back, and I walked out. I was mad. I called my pastor and told him what had happened. He said, "He heard that this pastor was like that."

Then one of the mothers of my church came to me concerned about my uprooting and moving with Leonard out of state. I even had dreams about it. Do you think that stopped me? No. I went anyway. It wasn't until we moved there that God opened up my eyes and got my attention.

The last two years of my marriage with this man were way worse than this. I thank God for His protection over Dillon and me.

We had moved in with his mother and brother. We stayed there for a few months. While we lived there, I watched his mother pit him and his sister against each other. In other words, they would be into it. His sister lived below us. She and I used to get along. Then she started blaming me for Leonard being violent. It had nothing to do with me. Leonard had hardcore issues. He just didn't deal calmly with things.

We were going to church with a couple he had gone to school with. The former classmate stated that he was surprised to see Leonard in church due to in high school that Leonard threw a desk across the room. My eyes got big.

After a few months of us living with his mother, we moved into our own place 20 minutes away.

Things started back up to where Leonard was breaking things. This time he took a TV tray and busted the chandelier. Then it went from that to banging his head into doors, taking books, and hitting himself in the head. He even said that he had a code on the phone for long distance and that he would have to dial out for me. He would sit and listen to my calls.

Also, he told me that I wasn't allowed to go back home, not even for a visit.

I worked the third shift; he worked mostly Friday and Saturday nights. During the week he was supposed to have our son up and ready for school. He slept all night and day. He would be up late going to get Dillon from school. I was always afraid that Division of Family Services (DFS) would be called. I needed my sleep and Leonard slept all day. He was home at night.

We were attending church and made friends there. We lived next door to a friend of his that I particularly could not stand. This friend Rupert liked to stir up mess using the Bible, telling me I needed to be subservient to Leonard. I told Leonard he needed to talk to his friend. Eventually, I just quit participating in the Bible studies at our home.

I would just go and sit in another room and shut the door. I wasn't listening to that. Especially, since Rupert was living what he proclaimed to not be. I was tired of being put down. I had enough. I was tired of being called out of my name, and then called by evil epithets, which Leonard did constantly, calling me out of my name, telling me how stupid I was, using huge words and telling me to look them up in a dictionary, breaking my things, and said I couldn't sing. He bragged about singing this octave and that octave. He would be the first one to write a book and I was not. He made fun of the music I listened to. By this time my self-esteem was gone.

Our car was also gone. It quit working. We had no car and had to depend on rides to get to work.

The abuse did escalate. He would never stop. He said he was going to counseling, but honestly, I didn't believe him. Every time I came home, he had different diagnoses. Mind you, he has a degree in psychology and pastoral counseling. He knew how to manipulate.

One October day, the kids were out of school and my friend Lisa and I had taken our kids for pizza, play, and to get a toy. We had a great a day. The kids had a blast. I came home and found that Leonard was in a mood. I just couldn't take it anymore. I told him I had had enough.

It still didn't stop him.

I believe it was December of 1995, when I sent $40 to a friend and gifts for her children. I asked Leonard to mail it for me. Leonard knew what was in the card. Leonard left to mail off the package and card for me; he said he had $18 on him. When he came back, he said he had $58. He stole the $40 out of the card. My friend let me know she never received it. It was because Leonard took it.

January of 1996, I remembered prayer and consecration. I had prayed for two weeks asking God to make a miracle out of me by the end of the year.

Things kept on escalating. God, in the meantime, was preparing for me and Dillon to leave. I had no idea until God showed me.

One of the ways was He had shown me as I was sitting in church. I was still married to Leonard. God had shown me two visions. The same visions, but I was standing in two different spots. God showed me in the vision, I was thinner in the vision, like I am today, I had blonde curly hair, my dress was purple, white, and gold with glitter, and I wore gold glittery pumps. My husband was behind the pulpit. All I saw were his broad shoulders. In the first vision, I was standing on the floor as though I was being introduced, and in the second one, I was standing right beside my husband. Mind you I never saw his face. I said to the Lord, "I am married." Little did I know I was being uprooted into better?

Things kept on getting progressively worse, even to the point of being scary.

Leonard got mad at me for something, and my son was in the room. Leonard knocked me to the ground. He left and I tried calling someone. They were afraid to help me, because they did not want Leonard to retaliate.

Then Leonard kept on with his craziness. As I said it kept getting worse. He had gone to the church for help. They said they would help us one time and if that meant Leonard had to work three jobs flipping hamburgers, he would. The person telling him this was working that many jobs to meet the needs of his family. It made Leonard mad, and he was taking it out on me. He was angry.

During all of this God used a friend in my life, to show me the Word of God, in Malachi 2:13-17 (KJV):

[13] And this ye have done again, covering the altar of the Lord with tears, with weeping, and crying out, insomuch that He regarded not the offering any more, or receiveth it with good will at your hand.

[14] Yet ye say, Wherefore? Because the Lord hath been witness between thee and the wife of thy youth, against whom thou hast dealt treacherously: yet is she thy companion, and the wife of thy covenant.

[15] And did not He make one? Yet had he the residue of the spirit. And wherefore one? That he might seek a godly seed. Therefore, take heed to your spirit, and let none deal treacherously against the wife of his youth,

[16] For the Lord, the God of Israel, saith that he hateth putting away: for one covereth violence with his garment, saith the Lord of hosts: therefore take heed to your spirit, that ye deal not treacherously.

[17] Ye have wearied the Lord with your words. Yet ye say, Wherein have we wearied him? When ye say, Every one that doeth evil is good in the sight of the Lord, and he delighteth in them; or, Where is the God of judgment?

This passage broke me of my religious spirit that almost got me killed in this marriage that wasn't a marriage that God ordained.

As things went on, I continued to stress they were worse. It had gotten to the point that I had to bum rides to work at night. I worked the third shift. The boyfriend of one girl who worked second shift had given me a ride one night. He said to me, "They found a woman's body in the incinerator on the island. "I said to him, 'How do you know?'" He looked at me and said, "They found her bones." He smiled as he was saying this. I was freaked out, to say the least.

As I mentioned earlier, Leonard's sister Maria and I used to get along and how she turned on me and blamed me for Leonard's violence. One evening she and I broke out in a verbal war screaming bloody murder at each other through the phone. Leonard lay on the bed grinning as though this was funny, but it was not. He was always pitting people against me, then grinning about it.

One evening Leonard was acting weird, and one of the pastors came by to bring us eggs. Leonard had taken a bunch of Trazodone (it is a serotonin modulator that helps with mental balance). We took him to the hospital. Leonard always threatened suicide; he cried wolf a few times to manipulate me and freak me out. It wasn't that I didn't care, because I did. I was exhausted mentally and emotionally with his games. He had a Dr. Jekyll and Mr. Hyde personality. He was taken to the hospital. They took him in the back. They were looking at me funny, and I had my co-worker's boyfriend (the person who told me about the woman on the island whose bones he said were found in the incinerator) whispering in my ear about Leonard and me going to counseling. I refused to listen to him.

I was finally able to go back to where Leonard was, Leonard was grinning ear to ear as the nurse was rubbing his feet and giving me a filthy look, and the doctor screaming and yelling at me. Leonard once again lied about me. I had to persuade Leonard not to say anything to his family. I was afraid they would take my son. I had not done anything to this man. After we got home from the hospital, Leonard was well enough to go to Seven Elven and get food. He was fine. I was not; I was a mess. When he left, I threw my rings across the room. Then the very next day we went and picked up Dillon from Leonard's family. Then we went to the park so Dillon could play. Leonard looked at me and said, "This is how I want my family to be." I was sick to my stomach. I was finally done. I had to make a plan. I didn't know what to do or where to even begin. It took me three weeks to find someone. I was able to make an appointment with the Coalition Against Domestic Violence later in the month of November or early December. I did request if there was a cancellation I would like an earlier appointment. A cancellation did occur, and I was able to take the appointment. I was led to the coalition of the state I lived in at that time. I met with an attorney. She told me when you move to a new state after six months it becomes the home state of the child. With this being said, I realized, "If I leave the state with my child, I could be charged with Federal kidnapping charges." I cried. My son and I had only been there not quite a year and a half. I wanted to take my baby and leave.

Before it got to this point, I was at church helping out with bagels, Leonard following me around, wanting me to kiss him. I said, "No." I went upstairs to Sanctuary. I said to him I need paper to write on. I found it in his Bible, and he meant for me to see it. He had a pamphlet for Domestic Violence. I was so sick to my stomach. I wanted to throw up. I knew what he was up to. I left and went home. I went to the phone and I didn't know if I could call long distance due to the supposed code on the phone. I take my risk, able to call my dad. He answered. All of this was a miracle. It was huge. I didn't know if I would be able to call out and usually my dad wasn't home, especially on a Sunday. He pastored a church. I told him what was happening. He said, "You have had enough, and you need to come home." That was on a Sunday, and this is how God works. Then on Wednesday evening I had gone to work as I usually had done. I called home as I usually did. Leonard was going off on me telling me that, his mother said a monkey could do his job! It got to the point I hung up and went to the porch to pray. All I heard God say was, "I need to trust you." The next morning, I went home to Hell. I got there; Leonard was pissed off. My son was not ready for school. I was trying to deal with my son. Leonard got mad and went off on me, started yelling and screaming bloody murder at me about our son. Then he had me backed up against the kitchen wall, yelling at me to hit him. I have never hit him nor would I. I knew he was trying to get me to so he could have me arrested. He threatened to get an *ex-parte* to keep me there. I never told him that I was leaving. I didn't say a word. He left, and as soon as he did, I made a call to the person who was afraid to help me before. He told me you and your son are leaving today. Then he said don't keep your son from him. The part about my child I had to ignore. Are you serious right now? I took my son to his school informing the teacher that he would not be coming back to his school.

We came back home and got together what we could, and I was nervous and keeping in contact with friends I knew that I could trust. God had me be quiet. I found out that one of the teen girls at our church was afraid of Leonard. He kept eyeing her. I didn't know until the day of. This was not the first time.

My neighbor girl who worked second shifts all of a sudden called me. She asked if I was coming to work. I played it off and said, "Yes. I will be there." I knew what she was up to. God had me to calm at that moment.

Then by 4:30 P.M., our ride came and took us to where we needed to go. By the time Leonard had gotten home, we were gone. Dillon and I were on our way to a battered women's shelter. We had been asleep on the bus, but once we crossed the state lines, Dillon was all excited, the sun was shining, and I knew then we would be all right. We got to the shelter at 11:30 P.M. at night. But while on the bus, I was scared that Leonard would find me.

We were trying to get settled in the shelter as well as we could. It was not a place you really wanted to be. The following week I met with my therapist, and she said to me, "If you hadn't left within the week, you would not be here with us."

The threat that Leonard had made in the beginning of our marriage was, "If you ever leave me, I will declare you unfit and have you committed." The promise of that threat just began. He put out a missing persons report on us. I received a letter from the detectives stating that they wanted to make sure that I left on my own, and that my son and I were safe. I needed to go to the nearest police station and let them know that my son and I were safe. I was freaked out. I had to go and do it, because there was a nationwide alarm out for me and my son. It had to be stopped. At that point, I was in a battered women's shelter. Leonard was calling places and people leaving voice messages saying, "We fear that Beth left with Dillon.... blah blah." I was at my (adopted) parents when he called there and I almost picked up the phone — thank God I didn't. My dad did not allow him to go any further with the conversation. He came in and told me what he had said. My dad put a stop to it.

Also, I had filed another *ex-parte* to keep him away from me. It took three weeks. When I did go, I was in shock. The judge that I went in front of, number one, was my biological parents' judge who started their divorce. I thought he was ok. I thought wrong. He looked me straight in the face and said, "Your husband's lawyer has written a letter on your husband's behalf. You have a 90 percent chance of being extradited to a women's prison and your son going to DFS." I lost it. My ex-husband's threats had come to fruition. I could not function for two weeks. I was told by the shelter director that I had to get help because I couldn't function. I went to a doctor, and they put me on Ativan. It did not cure what I was going through. It just sedated me.

I remembered that I kept the card from the attorney whom I met with. I and my case manager contacted the coalition. The coalition had gotten an attorney for me. She was something else. I adored this woman.

She fought for me. She stood up for me. I thank God for the coalition.

I had a therapist at the shelter. She told me if I didn't leave when I did within the week, I would not be here.

God is a good God.

Despite me, God looked out for me and my son. I didn't want my son to grow up in that any further. I think it was before I left, I had completed a housing application where I had lived with my ex-husband before. The Lord was making a way before I even got back.

I am going to take a praise break right in the middle of this chapter. I praise and thank God for His goodness, His mercy, His grace, His protection, His provision, and His care for me and my son.

I give God all of the glory, honor, and praise to His name. Even in the midst of my problems and my emotions.

While Dillon and I were at the shelter, I had a dream about my ex-husband and the devil in the dream. The very next day the Sheriff's Department came to the door looking for me. I was served custody papers. I cried, because Leonard was doing what he set out to do. My case manager and I had to do an answer or something of that nature.

Then not too long after that, Dillon and I moved out of the shelter, and I let my attorney know. Once I got moved, she had gone to court on my behalf. She called me and asked me to sit down. Even though I knew it was a risk, she told me they had a warrant out for my arrest. I lost it. I cried. I called the First Lady. She and her friend Ms. Alicia had come over and prayed with me. At the time, I was an emotional mess, angry all the time, and I would lash out at those who were in my corner. I pushed people away not even meaning to. I was traumatized to say the least.

Also, Leonard would send paperwork to my biological mother and sister. I ask them to send it to my attorney. They refused. I had to inform my attorney. I do not know how he even obtained their addresses. I didn't have them. I was not close to my family. He used that against me in court, saying I couldn't get along with my family.

I could not understand why this man even hated me or what I had ever done. Was I a perfect person? No. No one is. I had to walk on eggshells around this man.

And as time went on the judge said that to stay the warrant, I would have to come to the state I left and bring my son. That summer I had to go twice. The devil is ugly. I at the time didn't have money. I had to call upon a few folks for help and an agency where the lady was hell bent on not helping me. But God had a different plan. I even had the coalition help me by talking with that person, but she was relentless and would not help me. She only wanted to provide a one-way ticket and not round trip. I gathered what I could from a few people. I had a little but not much, and went back to the agency. There was a different lady there who did approve me and my son. Not one way, but round trip. As I said, God has a plan. I went to get the tickets and I was grateful, but at the same time the ticket agent was a smart-aleck and said something about them helping me. I am thinking like they didn't fund all of this, but yet are taking all of the credit. I didn't say a word. I didn't like his attitude. I got my tickets and went on. I had too much going on to listen to somebody like that. One of the amazing things was when I got back to one of the girls whom I love dearly at the church I attend still today, she approached me and said that the Holy Spirit had her praying for me. I cried. God was in all of this.

Another friend saw me as strong. I did not. I was about to break. I cried a lot. I was constantly looking over my shoulders, wondering at any moment if Leonard was going to find me. Others saw strength in me that I could not see. I was broken. I went to therapy off and on.

I had to go back to court in the other state not once, but twice that summer. The first time, Dillon had to stay for two weeks with Leonard; I cried for the two weeks. I didn't want to leave Dillon there. Leonard's brother and sister-in-law were there on Leonard's behalf. I had the coalition and my attorney and advocate there for me. I was scared. It bothered me that Leonard would do this. I just didn't and still don't understand the lengths that someone would go to just to destroy and tear another person down.

Through all of this, I was crazy enough to want to go back to Leonard. I began to pray. I asked the Lord to help me, by fixing it. I had to talk to Leonard about Dillon. I had the nerve to tell Leonard I wanted to come back. He already had someone else. We were not even divorced yet. I knew it was God's way of protecting me from me. Anytime I had to talk to Leonard by phone regarding our son, he would make snide comments, like, "You don't need the coalition backing you up, and you need a psychiatrist." "Dillon needs to come and live with me," I replied to Leonard, "you're nothing but a vacation spot." I dreaded talking to Leonard.

I had to re-establish residency where I currently live after six months. Then I was able to file for my divorce. In the midst of it, the attorney I was given had taken another position as attorney in a different court, so I didn't have him anymore and I had to obtain another attorney. Eventually, I got my divorce. I was so glad it was over. It was two years of craziness. Leonard refused to pay me any child support until the divorce. He only gave me 75 dollars in the two years. When Dillon visited Leonard for the summer, and they had a birthday party for Dillon. He would come back with over two hundred dollars. I had to tell Dillon I am not competing with that. I had birthday parties for Dillon. I did my best.

There were times I had it together and there were times I did not. I was an emotional mess. God had to heal and deliver me from depression. For a few years, when Dillon had to go see Leonard for Christmas, Spring break, and summer, I would cry, and I would lose my keys. Because I was that stressed out, and worried about Dillon. I had Dillon in therapy too. The counselors would say he was doing fine, but when it was just us, he would react differently. As his mother I knew they were wrong.

It took me 16 years to forgive Leonard for all that he had done. It took the grace of God. I was so devastated that my marriage failed. Truth is, my marriage wasn't a marriage to begin with. It was total horror.

Also, my mail from Leonard went to the church. I received a letter one day from him stating he had known where I had lived for over a year. I was freaked out and called my son's school. I spoke with the principal. He said if he comes here, I will call and have him arrested.

I took the letter and gave it to one of the ministers of my church. Eventually, I found out how Leonard had gotten hold of my address. I was not happy.

I went through a lot. People who are Christians would say to me, "He abused you because you were not meant to be together." Do not say that to people!!!!!

A friend of mine advised me to talk to my former pastor about what had happened.

That was a big mistake. He said I deserved it because we had fornicated before marriage. We did not have sex before marriage, and he didn't know what he was talking about. Here again, it goes back to Leonard going to his class and telling whatever he told. I thank God for my pastor, my bishop whom I currently have, who has been in my corner this whole time. He does not look down on me for any reason. Yet he is so loving and kind toward me and my son. He has never said one thing out of line to me about anything.

This isn't my entire story about my marriage, there is a lot more to this. But to God be the glory. I am more than a survivor. I am victorious. All the nay sayers in the world do not have anything on the God I serve. He will show out and show up for me.

God has the last say, not man. Through all of this, I know God as my protector and healer and provider.

Chapter 3 - Lack of Trust

The Merriam-Webster Dictionary says a lack of trust or confidence is a feeling that someone or something is not honest and cannot be trusted.

I John 4:18 says, *"There is no fear in love, but perfect love casts out fear. For fear has to do with punishment, and whoever fears has not been perfected in love." (ESV)*

The scripture above speaks volumes to me. This was a wall I had built up. The lack of trust has cost me a lot. It was based on fear. I have had many good relationships that have suffered due to me not being able to trust. Along with this goes the root of rejection.

The definition of rejection is when you feel excluded or not accepted. This was me. I have always felt like the outsider. Regarding my family, I have felt like the black sheep of the family. When I was 18 years old and left home, my father disowned me. I believe it was because I didn't take his side in the divorce between him and my mother. Also, I wasn't going to be there to take care of my brothers and keep up the housework. I have felt like my father had disowned me years prior to my leaving.

I allowed the hurt and pain of my past to stunt me for the longest time. I didn't know how to rise above it. That is why I went to counseling. I knew I needed the help. I knew that if I didn't, I would not go anywhere in life. I wanted to know how to overcome this problem and live a full and productive life. I wanted more than how I had to live, and I didn't want to stay in a dysfunctional home. I would not have made it if it wasn't for the Lord on my side.

A lot of my issues were with my father after the age of eight. Before the age of nine, I felt that I was daddy's little girl, but when an event I have already mentioned in my book happened, after that was when I felt I wasn't daddy's little girl anymore. He looked down upon me with great disgust and made fun of me. That was the pain that the Lord had to deal with me about. I forgave my father for it.

Ephesians 6:4 says, "Fathers, do not provoke your children to anger by the way you treat them. Rather, bring them up with the discipline and instruction that comes from the Lord." (NLT)

My mother forsook me. I knew she had no love for me. This was deep rooted for me. I wanted my mother to love me. She didn't. I was 14 years old when she was screaming bloody murder at me, yelling, *"I HATE YOU AND WISH YOU WERE DEAD!!!!!"* That hurt me to the core of my bones. I couldn't understand how she could hate me as much as she did. I don't know what I had to do for her to feel this way. It definitely strained our relationship. I couldn't trust her. I didn't like being in the same room with her. Again, I have forgiven her.

Psalms 27:10 says, *"Even if my father and mother abandon me, the Lord will hold me close."* (NLT)

My relationship with my now ex-husband wasn't good from the beginning. I can't go back.

He hurt me through and through. It was not only me, but also our son. Once I got married it was supposed to be until death did us part. In other words, our marriage was supposed to last forever. That was not the case. My dreams were shattered. I never thought in a million years this would happen to me. The relationship was a violent relationship. I never understood why he would marry me if he had no love for me and also bring a child into the mix. I love my son. I never wanted my son to go through all that I had to go through as child. That is why I took a risk, taking my son and fleeing.

Malachi 2:14 says, *"You ask, 'Why?' It is because the Lord is a witness between you and the wife of your youth. You have been unfaithful to her, though she is your partner, the wife of your marriage covenant."* (NIV)

Malachi 2:15 says, *"Has not the one God made you? You belong to him in body and spirit. And what does the one God speak? Godly offspring. So be on your guard, and do not be unfaithful to the wife of your youth.* (NIV)

Malachi 2:16 says, *"The man who hates and divorces his wife,"* says the LORD, the God of Israel, *"does violence to the one he should protect,"* says the LORD Almighty. So be on your guard, and do not be unfaithful. (NIV)

Malachi 2:17 says, *"You have wearied the LORD with your words. 'How have we wearied him?' you ask. By saying, 'All who do evil are good in the eyes of the LORD, and he is pleased with them' or 'Where is the God of justice?'"* (NIV)

The passage of scripture above was where the Lord had freed me. I lived in such a spiritually skewed view. I was living religiously and not in the relationship with God that I should have been. I didn't think I could leave my husband due to being abused. I was messed up. God doesn't want us to stay in an abusive relationship of any kind. Sometimes religious people don't have a clue. They are living religiously and not relationally.

The God I serve doesn't want his daughter to be abused. I don't care what title you hold in the church. I have had other Christians say to me, *"The reason he abused you was because you weren't supposed to be together."* This is a totally misguided statement if I have ever heard one.

At first, I was out done. The person who said it to me was close to me. I was like "wow!"

There were other comments said as well by others. Sometimes as Christians we do make mistakes. We have to be mindful in what we say when people are going through hard times. It doesn't mean walking on eggshells. Some of what comes out of our mouths needs to be taken back to the altar and crucified.

All of this being done and said to me kept me bound for years. As I have said, I had built walls to keep others out. But once I started dealing with things, the walls started coming down. It was frightening at first. I was closed off and didn't want to share. I was afraid and didn't trust anyone. Not even God. But once I allowed God in, then amazing things started happening.

I am able to trust more than I ever have. Also, I am wiser in the fact I know what I will and won't take from someone, either. Today, I know who I am more than ever. Each day gets better and better. God does love us. He doesn't want His children to be hurt in any way, shape, or form. He is our shield, our protector, and our buckler. God is love. We can trust Him. He is not a man that He should lie.

Chapter 4 - STRONGHOLDS

Merriam-Webster Dictionary says the definition of a stronghold is a place of security or survival.

Due to all the things that I have endured in my life, I put walls up, to keep others out as a way to protect myself. As a result, I kept God out, too. What this did for me was keep me bound and not free. God wasn't able to reach me, because of the wall I had placed there. Therefore, I was closed off and distant from those whom I needed the most.

The stronghold that I had built began in my mind. I had a wrong perception of who God is and who I am in Him. I grew up believing that our parents were examples of who God is. When your parents are abusive and neglectful, you have a different point of view. For many years as a young person, especially in my teen years, I thought God hated me and didn't want me. My thinking was very messed up. I couldn't think of God as a loving and kind God.

Also, I didn't like who I was. I thought I was a nobody. The record playing constantly in my head said, "You won't amount to anything." "You are worthless." "You are fat." "You are ugly." "I hate you and wish you were dead." What was I supposed to think? My perception of God and me were all messed up. I wasn't told, "I love you! "And I wasn't told I was pretty. I wasn't told, "You did a great job" So, I automatically I believed the lies that were told to me constantly. This is where I began to build the walls. I was shamed and rejected-based.

For many years I was just trying to survive to make it in this life. When I was 16 years old, I had a teacher say to me, "If you don't like and love yourself, then no one else can." At that time, I didn't know what she meant. Today I do. I was in constant emotional pain. I was struggling and didn't know what to do.

I had an incorrect perception of who God is. I thought God was this harsh deity and didn't want and no part of whom I was. In all realty God is a God of love. In I John 4:16 it says, *"We know how much God loves us, and we have put our trust in his love. God is love, and all who live in love live in God, and God lives in them."* (NLT)

I had a wrong perception of who I was in God. As I said, I felt shame-based, unworthy of God's love; I had low self-esteem; I didn't like myself; I had a guilt complex; and due to what had happened to me as a child, I felt shame and guilt that carried into my adulthood. I felt like I was the black sheep of my family. I didn't know how to have a relationship with God, let alone with anyone else, including myself.

I have learned along the way that God does love me and is not ashamed of me. God's love covers a multitude of sins. He sent His Son Jesus to the cross to pay the price for all of our sins. Jesus bore it all. We don't have to listen to the lies of Satan our enemy. He was defeated when Jesus rose from the dead and descended to Hell and took the keys and then ascended to Heaven to sit at the right hand of God. The devil is a liar. He continues to use his old tricks. If we don't know who we are in Christ, we will fall for it.

I felt so condemned by people and myself. Romans 8:1 clearly says, *"So now there is no condemnation for those who belong to Christ Jesus."* (NLT)

No one has the right to condemn another person or ourself. This is not God. If we don't know who we are in Christ, the enemy will run with this, if we let him. We have a choice to say "no" to the devil. We don't have to listen to his lies.

As I wrote this book, the Lord spoke to me about the strongholds in my life.

The strongholds began at age nine. This was the defining moment when the boy who lived up the street had his way with both my sister and me. I got a beating from my mother, and my father laughed at me and called me, "Weedzee." My sister didn't get the beating and called out of her name and laughed at. This is where things started. God showed me the following.

1. My mother caused the rift between my sister and me.
2. My father never looked at me the same. I became the black sheep of the family. Before this happened, I used to sit on the arm of the chair by my dad. When this happened, nothing was the same. I was nine years old.
3. As a result of this, for many years, I was so angry at life, at my parents, and even God. I couldn't understand what would make your mother hate you so much. What would make your father not even look at you anymore. There was no love. I ended up being depressed for many years. I was oppressed. I didn't know how to deal with this. I did the best I could. This wasn't something you talked about. It took me time, but eventually I forgave them both. I never had a relationship with my mother. When she passed, I lost it. We didn't have a relationship. I didn't get what my sister had with her. I eventually got over that, too. The Lord has blessed me to heal. With my father, I have tried, but it is the same old condemning thing. The conversation is

always negative. I had to cut the relationship and I choose to love him from a distance. What I have learned over the years is you can forgive someone, but you don't have to go back for more. I chose not to.

4. The other things I have learned about me I am able to admit now: I worry about what others think of me. This is what I am asking God to deliver me from. It is not easy to live like this. It affects my life. I don't and I choose not to live like this. I know God is a healer and a deliverer. He has done so much for me already. He will heal and deliver me from this, too. I thank God in advance.

It isn't that people don't want to do right. They have had a hard time of letting go of the pain, as well as the person who caused the pain.

It is easier to tell someone to let things go, especially when you are not the one living in the pain.

The power of God will save, sanctify, heal, protect, and deliver us.

Psalms 34:19 says, *"The righteous person faces many troubles, but the Lord comes to the rescue each time."* (NLT)

Chapter 5 - Anger

The biblical definition of anger is the righteous indignation is typically reaction emotion of anger over mistreatment, insult, or malice of another. In some Christian doctrines, righteous anger is considered the only form of anger that is not sinful, e.g., when Jesus drove the money lenders out of the temple (Gospel of Matthew 21).

https://en.wikepedia.org>wiki>Righteous_indignation

Anger is injustice is a healthy spiritual response. Anger helps us see what is wrong and can motivate action to create positive change in the world. This sort of response creates a blessing rather than a curse. But anger can also reflect and intensify our wounds and separation.

http://bodymindsoul.org,spirituality

Common roots of anger include fear, pain, and frustration. For example, some people become angry as a fearful reaction to uncertainty, fear of losing a job, or fear of failure. Others become angry when they are hurt in relationships or are caused pain by close friends.

www.markmerrill.com

Words have great power. The anger I felt wasn't godly anger. As I write about the type of anger I had, I am not making excuses for it. I had a child of rage in me like no other. I didn't know how to deal with what had happened to me. The pain that I felt — hurt, betrayal, rejection, and abuse in my childhood and adulthood — for a while had control over me.

I felt no one loved me or cared for me. The negative words that had been spoken over me by those whom I trusted (my mother and my father, and ex-husband, among others) hurt me to my core. I was a child when the negative words were spoken over me into adulthood. Not only did I feel rejected, betrayed and hurt, but I felt replaced. I have been the black sheep of my biological family for years. My wounds were deep rooted.

I had built walls to protect myself. When I built these walls, I shut not only people out, but God, too. I never meant to, but I was afraid to let anyone in. I wasn't going to allow anyone to hurt me again. People did hurt me — those closest to me. I did not know how to receive genuine love. Those who were closest to me and trying to love me, I shut out. They were the ones to get the brunt of my anger. Not those who did the actual hurting. It isn't fair to those who really love me.

I had been rejected over and over. A person can only take so much of that. In life the reality is we will face rejection, but not from everyone. The hardest thing for me was the words spoken over my mind over and over. "You will amount to nothing!" "You are fat and ugly!" "I hate you and wish you were dead!" "If a woman can't take a hit now and then…!" "I will be the first one to write a book — you won't!" "You can't sing! Sing this octave and that octave!" "You don't need the coalition backing you up, you need a psychiatrist!" Some of these words were spoken over me; after they were spoken, I was laughed at by my own father. The most hurtful part is that my father and ex-husband claim to be men of God.

That hurt me the worst. I took my anger out on God. I am ashamed to say this, but at one point I shook my fist at God. I couldn't believe I did that. An angry person usually does things out of their character that you wouldn't expect them to do. Anger when not dealt with can be deadly —not just physically, but also mentally and spiritually.

At 17 years old, I was diagnosed with chronic depression. The depression was situational, but ongoing. This is due to anger turned inward. For many years, I wondered what I had done that was so bad. I lived this way for a long time. I wasn't able to smile; I wasn't able to enjoy life. I didn't know how to relate to others. I thought everybody hated me, that

I was an unlovable person. At the time, truthfully, I wasn't. I didn't realize that then as I do now.

I wanted to be free; I wanted to live my life to the fullest but didn't know how then. In November of 2015, I was delivered from depression. I had lived with depression for over 30 years. God set me free. I am blessed and grateful that God set me free. God had spoken to me that night about my mindset. That He (God) cannot pour new wine into old wineskins. In other words, your mindset has to change.

Romans 12:2 says, *"Don't copy the behavior and customs of this world, but let God transform you into a new person by changing the way you think. Then you will learn to know God's will for you, who is good and pleasing and perfect."* (NLT)

God gives us choices. Everything begins with a thought, whether negative or positive, and then there is a chemical release, an emotion, and a reaction. Every day when we wake up, we need to make a decision about how our day is going to be. Regardless of what goes on, we are to put on the mind of Christ. We are to put on the full armor of God. (Ephesians 6). Without God, life is impossible to live.

I am still working on this. Sometimes I do well, and other days are rougher. The Bible says in Luke 1:37, *"For the Word of God will never fail."* (NLT)

Ephesians 4:26 says, *"And 'don't sin by letting anger control you. Don't let the sun go down while you are still angry.'"* (NLT)

I had a right to be angry, but the way that I handled my anger was wrong. It wasn't of God. I praise God that I have overcome it. Only by God's grace have I. Anger has affected me in terrible ways. Not only did anger affect my relationships with people close to me, but God, and other areas of my life. Hurting people hurt people. Unfortunately, it is the ones who truly do love you that get the brunt of you.

Do I have regrets? There have been many times I have had regrets. I have lost people in my life due to anger. People are only going to deal with that for so long. Then they walk away. Not everyone will, but there will be some. You will have to apologize, change, let people be, and move on. Forgive yourself. God does. Don't stay there. God doesn't. God wants you to be free.

That is why He sent Jesus to die on the cross for us. To destroy what the enemy tried to do to you and that was to destroy you.

God is forgiving. He forgives us. John 8:3–11 says, *"(3) The scribes and the Pharisees brought a woman who had been caught in the act of adultery, and placing her in the midst (4) they said to him, 'Teacher, this woman has been caught in the act of adultery. (5) Now in the Law, Moses commanded us to stone such women. So what do you say? (6) This they said to test him, that they might have some charges to bring against him. Jesus bent down and wrote with his finger on the ground. (7) And as they continued to ask him, he stood up and said to them, 'Let him who is without sin among you be the first to throw the stone at her.' (8) And once more he bent down and wrote on the ground. (9) But when they heard it, they went away one by one, beginning with the older ones, and Jesus was left alone with the woman standing before him. (10) Jesus stood and said to her, 'Woman, where are they? Has no one condemned you?' (11) She said, 'No one, Lord.' And Jesus said, 'Neither do I condemn you; go, and from now on sin no more.'"* (ESV)

Don't allow naysayers to turn your world upside down. As a child you can't defend yourself, but as an adult you can, and you can change the negative words spoken over you, by filling yourself with the Word of God, prayer, counseling, and inner healing. This for me has not been overnight. It has taken many years for me to get past my trauma. I still work on it. Every day we live in this world, there will be issues that rise up. Now we have the tools to overcome what comes our way.

Inch by inch, I have overcome many obstacles in my life. By the Grace of God there go I. Without God it is hard to live. We can't be apart from God and live a good life. God is my anchor, my father, my friend, and my everything. **"GOD WILL NOT HURT YOU. HE CAN'T. HE IS A GOD OF LOVE, NOT HATE, NOT DESTRUCTION, NOT ANGER, NOT MALICE, NOT RAGE, NOT IMPATIENCE; HE DOES NOT THROW US AWAY AS OTHERS HAVE."**

Chapter 6 - Anxiety

The biblical definition of anxiety is an uneasy feeling of uncertainty, agitation, dread or fear. The Bible often renders these words as thought, worry, or care. The Bible often depicts anxiety as the common human reaction to stressful circumstances. (Baker's Evangelical Dictionary of Biblical Theology https://www.biblestudytools.com/dictionaries/bakers-evangelical-dictionary/)

Growing up I had to live a life of uncertainty. I didn't know whether or not I would get slapped across my face, screamed at by my mother or beaten by her. With my father it was always the name calling or how disappointed in me he was. It wasn't once in a while, but all the time. I never knew when things were going to blow. I had to walk on eggshells all the time. I was always afraid, of my mother.

Being the oldest I worried about my family. I often worried about one of my brothers, who was in addiction at age ten, and eventually died at age forty-one. Living in a dysfunctional family you have to take on responsibilities you shouldn't have to take on. For me it was the child being the parents while the parents were acting like the child. In this case it was for me. I had to be the parent before my time.

I was young and worried all of the time. I wondered what would tick my mother off today for her to smack me, yell at me, and humiliate me in front of my friends. I worried about what we would eat or if we would have clean clothes, due to my mother rarely being there. There were times she had worked.

My mother wasn't there for us. A lot of times we were home by ourselves. As early as age nine, I recall when I noticed both my parents not being there for us kids. I never knew where my mother was, and my father would always be at my grandmother's. When we were left alone bad things did occur.

My father had left his BB gun on the bed in the living room, with the safety off. My brother a little younger than me got mad at me and aimed the gun at me and shot me in my temple. I had just turned my head or he would have shut my eye out. My father was at my grandmothers and I called him and he came home briefly checked on us and left again. Nothing had gotten resolved.

The older I got didn't get any better. I had to take on more responsibility than I should have. My life, as a child and a teenager, was taken from me. While my mother was a stay-at-home mother, she did nothing. She would either be sitting in the dark, in a chair, in the living room, with her knees to her chest, eyes closed, cigarette in her hands, off into another world.

Another time I had come home at lunchtime to ask for more money for lunch because my brother took it from me. I had a friend from school with me, my mother was passed out on the couch and I told her what happened and she screamed bloody murder at me and my friend and I left. I was embarrassed.

I felt like I was my mother's little slave. She never cleaned the house, but always demanded I do, my brother and sister never had to do anything. If I didn't, she would threaten to tell my dad. It didn't matter whether or not I had homework. My mother used intimidation because she knew it would work for me. I was petrified of her. If I didn't do what she said, I was afraid I would get screamed at or beaten by her. I lived in sheer terror of this crazy person. She didn't like me no way.

There were times I really wondered if I were hers or my father's child as much as they mistreated and hated me. My mother's constant yelling, my father's berating comments, and my ex-husbands abuse of me paved the way to fear and anxiety for me. I trusted no one.

I had built walls around me to keep people out. It was a way of survival for me.

Even though I wanted to let people in, I wasn't able to. I was scared of being hurt. I was worried, if someone started to know me they wouldn't like me.

Sometimes that did happen. The perception I had of myself was, "I am no good." No one is going to love me. I fed into that fear, worry, self-sabotage, anxiety, and other stressors. I at the time didn't know any different.

Even in my marriage, I had to walk on eggshells. At the beginning of my marriage, my ex-husband said to me, "If you ever leave me, I will declare you unfit and have you committed." It came out of nowhere. We were just going down the road when he said this. No arguments, no nothing. I never knew when he would go off or even what about most of the time. Whatever mood he was in you had to try and flow with it, but sometimes that didn't even work. He was like Dr. Jekyll, Mr. Hyde.

There were a lot of threats made toward me. A lot of choices he wanted me to make or else. I was made to choose between him and the church. I chose the church because I knew God first. He got up, went into the kitchen, got a knife, and lay down on the ground with the knife between his armpit, hollering. I looked at him what the heck. There was no reason for this.

Another time he wanted me to choose between him and my job. He said if I didn't quit my job our marriage was over. I didn't quit my job.

There were constant demands and threats. My nerves were wrecked and I was hanging on for the sake of my son. Daily I worried about how I was going to get treated. What if I get this wrong or say this wrong? What is going to happen to me? I was always stressed out. I felt there was no way out. For me I felt there was no protection. I was afraid of my own shadow. I felt if I relaxed or tried to get comfortable, the rug would be pulled out from underneath me. Usually, it did. God doesn't intend for me to live this way. God doesn't intend for anyone to live like this.

Finally, the day came and I took my son and fled. My ex-husband tried to do what he said he would do at the beginning of our marriage. He tried getting, an ex parte against me, and when I did flee; he did put out a missing person's report on both my son and I. Calling my friends and my adopted family trying to seek me out. He would have his attorney mail out important paperwork sent to my mother and sister and they wouldn't send it to my attorney. He was able to get their addresses and I didn't even have them. He did what he could to what he set out to do toward me.

Then a year later I receive a letter from him, where I was receiving my mail from him. He wasn't allowed to know where I lived but he found out later. I had taken my son to the dentist I told them he was not to know my address. When they filed the insurance, the insurance company allowed him to have my address. I was not happy. I reported the issue. I ended up giving the letter to one of the ministers in the church

In the end, he didn't win. I was facing time in prison for fleeing the state with my son. God blessed me in the court system. I didn't go to prison and I was awarded custody of my son. I got my divorce finalized two years later. From there my life keeps going up and upward in God. I have forgiven all of the ones who have hurt me.

I John 4:18 says, *"There is no fear in love, but perfect love cast out all fear, because fear involves punishment, and the one who fears is not perfected in love."*

I Peter 5:7 says, *"Casting all of your anxiety on Him, because He cares for you."*

Psalms 55:22 says, *"Cast your burden upon the Lord and He will sustain you. He will never allow the righteous to be shaken.*

Zephaniah 3:15 says, *"The Lord has taken away His judgments' against you; He cleared away your enemies. The King of Israel, the Lord, is in your midst, You will fear disaster no more."*

About three years ago I was in a car accident. My car was totaled. Before the accident I was driving out of town. I enjoyed it. After the wreck, I wasn't able to make myself go very far. It caused me to miss out on a wedding I wanted to attend so badly. But because of the fear, I couldn't make myself go. I felt bad. It almost took a toll on me. I still go through things when driving. I am way more cautious than before. I do not like people coming from behind me. I can't look when cars approach. That is how frightened I become. People who know me know so. For the longest time I didn't want to drive anywhere. I didn't feel safe and at times I have to admit that I don't. It used to be a chore to drive. Over time I have gotten better with driving. Like I said, "I still get nervous and have anxiety." I have to fight it daily. There are times I am real comfortable and other times I am not. A lot of times I do take side roads. I will get off the main roads when there is too much traffic. I do what I have to do for me. The Lord is stretching me a little bit. Bit by bit. I have had to travel outside my city a lot lately. I take the way that is comfortable for me.

I praise God that there is more than one route to a place.

What I have to do is pray and ask for God's hedge of protection around me. I praise God for taking me to and fro and getting me to my destinations safely and my home safely. I don't take it for granted.

I know too many people who have been in car accidents since. It is wild the amount of people I know. I allowed fear to set in. It had me for a while. I didn't go to church for a little while. Anxiety and fear will do a lot to you. This isn't of God. The enemy will do what he can to stifle you.

Everything that has happened to me will never keep me from serving God. Has it detoured me? For a bit it did, but then I picked up myself and tried again. God is good. I didn't get mad at God. I knew where this came from. The one thing I know the enemy is always busy with his job and doesn't miss a beat. We have to be on ours too. With God we are not defeated. Our last words aren't defeat, but we win. God's promises are yes and amen.

If you get knocked down and trust me you will. Don't stay down. Get back up fight. We will always go through something. But it is how we handle it as to whether or not we are victorious. Am I perfect? No, but I strive daily with the help of the Lord to do my best.

Psalms 34:19 says, *"The righteous person faces many troubles, but the Lord comes to the rescue each time."* (NLT)

Psalms 34:19 says, *"Many are the afflictions of the righteous, but the Lord delivers him out of them all."* (ESV)

Chapter 7 - UNFORGIVENESS

The definition of unforgiveness according to the Merriam-Webster Dictionary is unwilling or unable to forgive or having or making no allowance for error or weakness.

For many years I was unwilling to forgive those who hurt me. I was a severally depressed person. I was diagnosed with Chronic Depression at the age of 19 years old and God delivered me when I was in my late 40s. I was in bondage to depression for many years. During these years of my life, I had been suicidal, unhappy, had no joy, no peace, couldn't sleep, and had other symptoms.

The root of unforgiveness in my life came from the household I had to grow up in. There was a lot of abuse. All through the book I talk about the abuse I had suffered at the hands of my mother and father. It had taken me years to forgive them for what they had done to me. Even though my mother is now gone and my father is still alive, our family never has come together.

Also, I was in an abusive marriage that nearly had taken a toll on me. But the Lord blessed me to escape that marriage with my life. I talk about my marriage as well. It took me 16 years to forgive him for what had happened.

It isn't that I haven't tried to work things out with my father, but every time we tried it didn't work. He hadn't changed and I have. We would do ok for a while and then he would say the same things all over again and I would get upset. I made the decision that I no longer could do this for my health. It is the same things with my brothers. Even with my brothers I would get just as bad as they would. To have peace I just stay away from them. Our family didn't have a strong family foundation to begin with. It isn't that I don't believe that can God can heal and deliver us, sometimes you just have to back away and let people be.

When you are unable to forgive it comes with a price and a horrible price at that. This is not what God wants. As Christians, we are required to forgive. God has forgiven us, so we must forgive. It isn't for the person you're holding the unforgiveness toward, it is for you.

When you are an unforgiving person it weighs on your mind, hurts your soul, and affects your attitude, and your health.

"Online according to John Hopkins, when you have chronic anger, it leads you into fight or flight mode, which results in numerous changes in your

heart rate, blood pressure, and immune response. Those changes then increase the risk of depression, heart disease, and diabetes, amongst other conditions. Forgiveness, however, calms stress levels, leading improved health."

Regarding unforgiveness, in these relationships it caused me to not trust. There was a time when I wasn't able to trust God. There were times I felt God was the same way. Thankfully I found out that was a lie. My belief systems and what I believed were skewed. There were many days I didn't know whether I was coming or going. I was in deep rooted pain, in which I thought would never go away. By the grace of God, it has. I am so thankful for that.

Unforgiveness not only affects you, but those who are around you. Your family, your friends, and others.

Chapter 8 - INSECURITIES

The definition of insecurity is as follows: A state or feeling of anxiety, fear, or self –doubt. (Merriam-Webster Dictionary https://www.merriam-webster.com/). Biblically, insecurities are the lies we believe about ourselves. All of those lies, that others have spoken over us, we received and accepted them. Those words of others are not to allow attachment to us. When you are a young child, when it comes from family, those who are supposed to love you, that spouse who is supposed to love you, that friend who is supposed to love you, coworkers, bosses, and instead of believing what God says about you then you dismiss Him and take on what the others have said about you that is not true. God is not a God of lies; the devil is. If the devil can get your mind, he can get your emotions, your belief system, and take you where you don't want to go. As Joyce Meyers wrote in her oft-quoted book *Battlefield of the Mind: Winning the Battle in Your Mind*, "The Mind Is the Battlefield." You have to stand up and fight with the Word of God, the Double- Edged Sword that will pierce the heart of man. The Word of God is our Truth.

In regard to insecurity, I can expound on this. In the past I didn't have the confidence I needed. There were many instances when I felt I was stupid and believed that lie. For many years and it starting as a young girl, being told, "You are worthless", "You will never amount to anything." "You are ugly" "You're fat." Then I was laughed at after it was said to my face. I was devastated and hurt. "You will never write the first book, I will." "You can't sing, sing this octave and that octave." People that were supposed to love me were my enemies. They were my immediate family members. It cut to the root of who I was. I lived like this for years.

I didn't like myself. I hated who I was and why I even existed. My life was hell. My father and mother wanted to be respected, but they always degraded us every chance they got. Family members can say what they want, because they were not there. They didn't live our hell. We were a very broken family that went in eight different directions, with our own hurt and pain.

I felt so stupid that in class I would never raise my hand. I didn't want anyone to know I was stupid. It was because I believed the lies that I was told about myself and who I was and was not. These words did a number on me. My father was someone who went to church and came home and would abuse us emotionally and think he was funny. No! I had to forgive my father for all of it. A few years ago, God told me I had to quit hanging the past over my father's head. I prayed, talked to the Lord, and went through a time of forgiveness toward him before I called him. I was really afraid of what he would say. To my surprise, it was different. That time, but God did that. I can't take credit for it nor can my father.

I have lived in anxiety long enough. I have lived in lack of trusting God long enough. I am done taking abuse from anybody. I am done not being confident.

God is the one who says who I am. Not man, regardless of who they are, that means us.

There were times my father who was very judgmental and critical would even doubt that I was even saved. He isn't God. One of my brothers has said that too. He has called me a liar and delusional. This should never be. Thankfully, I do not believe either one of them. Not any longer or anyone else who puts their mouth on me or others for that matter. Those are lies of the enemy. God doesn't treat us like we are stepchildren.

God says, in Romans 6:14, *"Sin is no longer your master, for you no longer live under requirements of the law. Instead, you live under Freedom of God's Grace."* (NLT)

Romans 8:37 says, *"No, despite all of these things, overwhelming victory is ours through Jesus Christ, who loved us."* (NLT)

We are more than conquerors through the blood of Jesus Christ. No man can take that away from you. My identity is in Jesus Christ, not man and what they say. I had to quit listening to the lies and dismantle those lies and read the Word of God and what God says about me.

I am chosen. I Peter 2:9 says, *"But you are A CHOSEN RACE, A ROYAL PRIESTHOOD, A HOLY NATION, A PEOPLE FOR God's OWN POSSESSION, SO that you may proclaim the excellencies of Him who has called you out of darkness into His marvelous light."* (NASB 1995)

I am redeemed. Isaiah 1:27 says, *"Let the redeemed of the Lord say so, Whom He has redeemed from the hand of the adversary."* (AMP)

Isaiah 44:23 says, *"Shout for joy, O heavens, for the Lord has done it! Shout in triumph, you depths of the earth; Break forth into jubilant rejoicing, you mountains, O forest, and every tree in it! For the Lord has redeemed Jacob and He shows His glory in Israel."* (AMP)

I am accepted. Ephesians 1:6 says, *"So we praise God for the glorious grace he has poured out on us who belong to his dear Son [Jesus]."* (NLT)

I am loved. John 3:16 says, *"For God so loved the world: He gave his one and only Son, so that* *everyone who believes in him will not perish but have eternal life."* (NLT)

I have an inheritance with Jesus. Romans 8:17 says, *"And since we are His children, we are his heirs. In fact, together with Christ we are heirs of God's glory. But if we are to share his glory, we must also share His suffering."* (NLT)

We as people do have a place in life. It does not matter what we have gone through, where we have been, what obstacles we have faced. We are all important to God. We matter, God does love us, and as (I have learned), God is not a monster. God is grace, He is mercy, He is love, He is peace, He is loving-kindness, He our protector (this one is huge for me); He is our healer and our deliverer. I do know all of this for myself.

The one thing I know about God, He is not ashamed of you or me. We are the apple of His eyes. When He looks at us, He smiles at us and is well pleased with His creation. Psalms 139:14 says, *"I will praise You, for I am fearfully* and *wonderfully made; Marvelous are Your works, And* that *my soul knows very well."* (NKJV)

God is so good. He has healed me, delivered me, and raised me up for such a time as this. Today, I can encourage myself in the Lord, when that was not always the case. I lacked a lot of confidence. God would show me things about myself that He loved about me. He showed me I was not stupid. God blessed me to go to college and get two degrees. The first degree I made the dean's list. I never ever made the dean's list in school before college. Not one time do I recall ever making the dean's list in high school. God showed me how beautiful I was and that I can overcome things in life.

God has placed me in situations to show me some things I could do, even when others doubted me, even when I doubted me.

God says who I am. Not my family, not my friends, definitely not my enemies, not evens me nor what you yourself say about you. The Bible tells us who God says we are. All through the Word of God it displays God's truths about you.

God loves us. God is real and not this monster. He is genuine. He loves us right where we are.

Chapter 9 - THE PURGING

In life, like anything else we must go through a process called purging. It isn't fun at all. I will not tell you that it is. But it is necessary to go through a purging to get past the pain of your past.

When the Lord first began to deal with me on purging, I wanted no part of it. It meant that I had to face me, my pain, and all that I had stuffed and not dealt with. I was afraid to face myself. It took me a long time to get to this point and allow God to come in and take over. I wasn't in denial; the pain was so great that I didn't want to deal with my issues; it kept me depressed, sick, and not able to function. I was of no use to God, me or anyone else. It was all due to being afraid to give over to the Lord.

The one thing I remember God saying to me is that He was not ashamed of me. I grew up in shame from a very young age. That shame caused me to suppress years and years of pain that I didn't want to face. When God said to me, "I am not ashamed of you," was when I knew I could trust Him and was willing to allow Him in. By this time, I was an adult.

Once I allowed God in and started allowing Him to purge me, I cried and cried and cried some more.

There was over 40 years' worth of pain that I had suppressed because I did not want to deal with it.

The one thing I love about the God I serve is He peels the layers off, little by little. He doesn't do it all at once. He knows that when we are facing us, that we need that time to process. He is the ultimate therapist.

As I began to deal with things, God always reassured me that He was with me. He would speak positive affirmations to me. God let me know my worth, value, importance, how much He loves me, and more. This helped me to process the pain and come to know God more.

Just to know that the God I serve loves me that much to whisper great things to me, while I was facing my pain. For me, knowing that there were angels around me, preventing the enemy, the devil, from trying to get to me.

Chapter 10 - FORGIVENESS

As I write about forgiveness. The Bible stresses the importance of forgiveness. It is the key to living a life of holiness, freedom, fruitfulness, and being able to move on from past pain and trauma.

Proverbs 17:9 says, *"Whoever covers an offense seeks love, but he who repeats a matter separates close friends."* (ESV)

I had a lot of forgiving to do. During this time of shelter in place, I began to seek the Lord. He has been talking to me this whole time. One of the people whom he brought to the forefront was my biological father. The Lord told me to quit hanging the past over my own father's head.

I want to backtrack some.

The relationship with my father had been strained for over 36 years. At the age of nine when I was molested, was where the separation between my father and I started. Especially, when he allowed my mother to beat me in front of him, he didn't stop her, and when he called me out of my name and laughed at me, this is where shame and guilt started. Before that I remember when I use to sit on the arm of his chair, and we would watch TV together. I thought I was daddy's little girl. When this all happened, I felt a ripping in my soul and I was hurting from that point on.

I was not able to hold my head up. I felt so much shame. I didn't like myself. I felt dirty on the inside out. I was damaged. No one helped me through this. I questioned. How could a father and mother show so much disdain toward their child?

God didn't just begin with me recently. The first time he had dealt with me, I was 25 years old. At that point I had condemned both my father and mother to Hell. Honey, no one has that right. I was playing God without realizing it. It wasn't what I was trying to do. I just had so much bitterness, anger, rage, hate, and self-hatred in me from what happened. I went through a time of consecration and honed into the Lord.

At the time, I thought I had forgiven them both. Years later, as a matter of fact, just recently, during this pandemic, God had spoken to me about not hanging the past over my father's head anymore. As a matter of fact, I had to call him and make amends. A year ago, I would not have visited this. I wanted nothing to do with him. Absolutely didn't want a relationship with him. I couldn't stand him. I forgave him, just not all the way.

I had for many years felt like the black sheep of the family. Any time I had gotten on the phone with him, it was always negative, and he was the grieving father of two deceased children. I just couldn't take that. I quit calling.

When God started dealing with me about it again, I obeyed Him and did what he asked. Currently I am in inner healing. I wanted to be obedient to God. I told God I didn't want to place anyone or thing above Him any longer. So, I watched the videos on forgiveness through inner healing and prayed before I made the call. Before I go on with this, my birthday was the month prior. I had received a birthday card with money in it. It was from my father and stepmother. They have never celebrated me or my birthday for that matter. When I received that card and opened it up, I sobbed.

Then I made the call to my father, and I explained to him that the Lord wanted me to call and make amends with him. I said to him, "God wanted me to stop hanging the past over your head. I told him I was sorry. My father said, "The past is the past, no judgment here. I love you like I love the boys. I can't come and see you due to my health, but I do want to see you."

You have to understand this is not the father I knew. He has always called me out of my name, always been critical of me. I couldn't do anything right. I allowed him to talk a little more and then I got off the phone and went into my bathroom and cried. God is a good God.

Chapter 11 UNWAVERING FAITH

Unwavering faith means that we trust God fully with ourselves. We do not doubt Him in the good and bad times in our lives. No matter what may be going on, we trust that God has everything in control. We do not have to worry about anything.

There were many times in my life that my faith had wavered, not being able to trust God. I had allowed the circumstances of life to overwhelm me. God had faith and confidence in me, but I didn't. I allowed what people said about me be my truth and not God's. God has the last say in our lives and not man. If we do not know who we are, anyone can come in and drag us around. This is what the enemy Satan wants. Satan wants us to agree with him. He doesn't have the power to overthrow us, unless we allow him to. Jesus overthrew Satan at the cross. Without realizing it, we have agreed with Satan by listening to the naysayers and ourselves, instead of listening to God and His truth about us. I Peter 5:8 says, *"Stay alert! Watch out for your great enemy, the devil. He prowls around like a roaring lion, looking for someone to devour."* (NTL)

Today, I am more convinced of how much God does love me and think of me often. There was a time in my life that I did not. It goes all the way back to my childhood. It actually took up root when I was age nine. There were some traumatic events that took place, which have tripped me up for many years. At one point in my life, I had thought God hated me. I believed that lie off and on. I was young and lacked a lot. My mindset was broken, my heart was broken. I grew up in shame, and criticism, made fun of by my father, hated by my mother. These things were hurtful. There were many times I wanted to end it all. I went into a deep-rooted depression. I lacked social skills due to my family life. I was in an abusive marriage that would have taken my life if I hadn't fled when I had. The people in my life had gone to church and still do. That was hard to digest in so many ways. A good friend once told me, "Stop looking at his life. It isn't what it seems." It took me a while to get there. Eventually, I did. "By the Grace of God there go I." God is the only reason why I live and have my being. I owe God my whole life. He sees me in a different life than me, the nay-Sayers, and others who may look down upon me.

For many years, even today, I feel like the black sheep of my biological family. I have forgiven them, but I don't want to go around them. Their talk, their walk, and their mindset have not changed. They want to rehash the old. If I am talking to them, guess what — so do I. I have to protect myself. That doesn't mean they're bad, they just haven't let go. God says I am not required to. I am not perfect. Sometimes in order to live, those things and people who once hurt you, you forgive them, but you don't have to go around for more punishment.

I am not saying I don't want them in my life; I just can't due to their negative mind sets. I have lived that life, and I am done. Sometimes our ego does have to be dealt with. Along with the ego is pride, unforgiveness, lack of love, lack of support, and lack of peace, lack of grace, lack of mercy, a hole in the soul, and pain that comes from the hole in the soul. God wants to deliver us, heal us, and make us whole. It is time for our deliverance. It is time for our Exodus. Our freedom is right here. God wants us free. While yet the enemy Satan does not. We serve a God who is higher than this. We have got to get rid of the stinking thinking and let God do what he needs to do. Without God it is hard to live, be at peace, have joy, freedom, and to be in a place of where He wants us to be.

Exodus means, "Freedom." This is what God wants for us. So many of us have been betrayed by others, such as our parents, (ex) spouses, church, work, and so forth. We can't use this as an excuse to detour our relationship with God. I have learned along the way that people are people and have failed us. On another note, so have we failed others. This is due to our humanness. To be able to overcome all of this, we must have unwavering faith in God. We must stop looking at everyone else and start checking ourselves. I am just as guilty. Once we surrender to God, He will help us turn it all around. He will bless us to overcome in areas we didn't think we were able to. His promises to us are true. Numbers 23:19 says, *"God is not man, one given to lies, and not a son of man changing his mind. Does he speak and not do what he says? Does he promise and not come through?"* (MSG)

God is for us and not against us. God knew who we were even before we were in our mother's wombs. He knows how many hairs are on our heads, He knows who we are because He created us to be. Sometimes we think differently than God does. The prime example, "When I got this promotion as a supervisor. I didn't want it. I have never wanted to be over anyone. I fought with God and fought with God. Did I win? **NO....** It goes back to my youth. The hell in my home life was enough for me. Back then I made an inner vow: "I never want to be a supervisor, because they are mean." What I was referring to were the adults in my life who were abusive and not kind to me. How I got that out of this, don't ask, because I don't know. I never thought in a million years I would be in this position. I never wanted to be. Still don't, but I am calming down about it. Me I love being behind the scenes. I don't need the spotlight nor do I ever want it. I am not about that. All I ever wanted to do was work in an office, do my work, and go home. I didn't want to think about people or things. I just wanted to work and go home.

But God says differently. This was my question to God, "Father, why can't I do something else? Is there another position besides this one? It is all based on fear. Trust me, people haven't been too nice. I have had a lot of naysayers. I have been hung upon the naysayers and what has been said about me. There has been some betrayal. Did it hurt me? Yes. You realize that people aren't really in your corner. In the back of my mind, I knew it. They are the type to throw rocks and hide their hands. If they wanted to, they could have had the position. They chose not to apply, but instead gossip, plot, and want to try and destroy good things in your life. When God is involved, they can't touch a hair on your head. Sometimes things will backfire in your face when you try and throw someone else under the bus. It isn't God at all. The funny thing is they knew I dreaded this position. They knew I didn't want this position, but yet they went to any length to try and destroy things in my life. God had to show me that I need to stop looking at them and focus on what He has called me to do. Yet I kept fighting with Him. Bishop has always told us what Black author and historian James Weldon Johnson said: "Your arms too short to box with God."

Apart from what was going on inside of me, I was listening to what people were saying about me, and I received some backlash. I walked in fear and lacked great confidence in my new position. I got so distracted with all of the naysayers and doers, that I lost sight of what God wanted to do in my life. I cried a lot. I have been overwhelmed with this position. I have never been a supervisor. This is where I have to rely upon God. I have no one else that will show me the way. I have had a lot of backlash. I am not a stupid person. Sometimes people who call themselves saved, but act the opposite. Act like they run the place. I've overheard someone say, "I am going to do such and such because I can." I started chuckling at that. I thought to myself, "Oh my, a little prideful aren't we?" I didn't say a word and went on.

It has been one test after another. My nerves have been a wreck. I had allowed the enemy in and made the agreement by not wanting to do what God says to do. God wants me to lead. Of course, me, I have been resistant, because I don't want to be in the front. I was told years ago by a great friend, "God says you need to get over your shy stage because your ministry is in the front." Of course, my reply back then was,

"You do two things: preach or sing. I do neither," and walked off.

I was Hell on wheels. I still can be. Am I proud of it? No. When I get something in my head, God will talk to me. "Now come on daughter turn it around. You are better than this. I didn't bring you this far to lose you." "I have great things for you." I am always praying, "God, I want to be the woman of God you have designed me to be." I really do, but never did I think it was being a supervisor. Honey, I wasn't content where I was before, but I am really not content where I am at right now, either. I know God probably shakes His head at me. I can be a bit of a challenge. I am not trying to be. My heart's desire is to please God. I do want to be all He wants me to be. I don't know better than God. He is all knowing. He created me. I am telling you regardless and in spite of myself, God genuinely loves me and cares about me. It goes for you as well. No longer will I allow my faith to waver concerning the things of God. He has not let me down. I have let Him down by allowing what people say and do regarding me get me down and you know what, no longer. I am ultimately responsible for me, not people. God, who is my Father, does think highly of me. It doesn't matter what other people think of me. I have to forgive and let all of that go. That doesn't matter. What God says will go and flourish while the naysayers stand back in disbelief. Jeremiah 29:11 says, *"For I know the plans that I have for you", declares the Lord, "plans to prosper you and not to harm you, plans to give you hope and a future."* (NIV)

Today is a good day for me and you to have our deliverance and Exodus. We are free and we are free in God. God says, "Take your life back. Don't allow the enemy in. Stop making an agreement with him. You are free and free indeed. I have not left you. I am not ashamed of you. I am not disappointed in you. Come home and let Me take care of you. Get back on your feet. I am here waiting." I love you, God.

Chapter 12 WORTH

Worth was an area of my life I truly struggled with. I felt stuck and had writers' block. I prayed, I cried, and nothing. I gathered a few prayer warriors to pray for me. The next thing I know, God blessed me. My prayer was answered, and I began to write. It flowed. I give praise to God.

When it came to worth, I hadn't felt I was worthy of love, especially God's love. It reflected my self-esteem, and how I viewed God, myself, life, and others.

As God had spoken to me, He told me to take it back to the Cross.

Our worth is not in things we have or what we do. It is in God.

For years I was told how worthless I was and that I wouldn't amount to anything, how stupid I was, I hate you and wish you were dead. This was embedded in me early on that I had no value or worth. This had come from my very own mother and father. In my marriage I wasn't valued either. My (ex-)husband made sure of that daily.

My ex-husband wanted me to know how much he devalued me as a person. He always called me crazy. Degrading me about the person I was as in what I liked, what I loved, and it nearly destroyed me. This is what he set out to do. At the very beginning of our marriage, he said to me, "If you ever leave me, I will declare you unfit, and have you committed."

All that has been said to me, as a child, teenager, and an adult weighed on me heavily. As a result, I put up walls, to keep those who hurt me out, but instead I shut God out, those who truly love me out, and walled myself in. Due to fear, I wouldn't allow God or anyone else in. I wanted to, but as I said I was afraid. God was who I needed.

It was hard, especially when the people who gave birth to me betrayed me, and didn't love me. One went to church, hiding behind his titles, as the superintendent of the church, Sunday school teacher, and Royal Ranger Leader, to a mother who was an addict and at the time it was unknown to me.

Then my ex-husband who had a BA in psychology and an MA in pastoral counseling, used intimidation, by using anger, looks, physical abuse, mental abuse, financial abuse, and spiritual abuse, among other abuse. No matter what I did it was never right. Being with him, I felt defeated before I even got started.

Things were already ingrained in me young. It was hard to escape.

My mother, who was an addict, was very cruel and cold hearted. She was the one who said, "I hate you and wish you were dead." I was very afraid of her. I worked and made my own money. When she used all of the money from my father's pay checks, she'd target me. When I told her I didn't have any, she would get mad at me and scream bloody murder. She then would call me a liar. I would end up giving it to her. I was afraid of this woman. If I didn't, she was prone to get physical. I usually went without because of her. This was how bad her addiction was. Back then I didn't understand a thing, and back then addiction was not talked about. But yet she would use her hollering to scare me into giving it to her. She hated me, I just don't know why. This has bothered me for years. I was a mess. I could never understand what or why she hated me.

My father was a belittler, and a yeller, and love to laugh in your face, and call himself a man of God. My father loved to taunt us, especially us girls. His issues were with females and still to this day are. He thought he could belittle us and berate us. My father's father was never this way. He was the exact opposite. I don't know where my father's issues came from.

My ex-husband would give me look and I didn't want to move, or he would come after me. He too was a belittler, berated me, let you know what he thought of me. It wasn't nice. He didn't only do this to me, but others.

The hardest thing for me was, I thought God was the same way.

Thankfully, I found out I was wrong.

It all goes back to what you identify with. I identified with the lies of the enemy and not what God said about me. It went to my belief system. Instead of believing God's Word about me, I believed my father, mother, and ex-husband. When you are raised in this, you don't know any difference.

Since I've been in the church I attend now, the First Lady has taught us, "You can't live any better than you know." This is a true statement. I have learned a lot from attending Transformation Hour, Bible Study, and Morning Service. I didn't get there overnight, and you never stop growing in the Lord. It is a daily process. I am still learning. Also, I still have more healing to do. What happened to me was not overnight. God is always in the healing business.

"Today, I truly do Thank God for that all He has done for me. God has helped me to come up and out of many things. What was meant to destroy me, God turned it around for my good.

"Your ministry comes out of your pain."

Hebrews 13:5 says, *"I will never leave you nor forsake you."* (ESV) We might feel displaced, not worthwhile, or devalued, and this is not of God. He created us for greatness and success. He tells us in Joshua 1:9, *"Have I not commanded you? Be strong and courageous. Do not be frightened, and do not be dismayed, for the Lord your God is with you wherever you go."* (ESV)

God does not hate; God doesn't belittle, berate, abuse, abuse, or torment; and He doesn't murder those He loves. All these things are not love.

When Jesus went to the cross, He went for us all. He paid a price we none could pay or repay. Romans 5:8 says, *"but God shows His love for us in that while we were still sinners, Christ died for us."* (ESV)

On the cross when Christ died, it was for our sins. It made salvation complete for us all. This showed God's love in a real huge way; it glorified God's love for us all. This is where our lives truly began. God's love, God's love is genuine. God wants a relationship with His children. When our own relationships fail, our relationship with God doesn't.

Psalms 139:13–16 says, *"For you formed my inward parts; you knitted me together in my mother's womb. I praise you, for I am fearfully and wonderfully made. Wonderful are your works; my soul knows it very well. My frame was not hidden from you, when I was made in secret, intricately woven in the depths of the earth. Your eyes saw my unformed substance; in your book were written, every one of them, the days that were formed for me, when as yet there was none of them."* (ESV)

If God didn't want us to be born, we wouldn't be. God wanted us born for His purpose, His glory, ultimately for a relationship with us God didn't reject us, throw us away. God has no throwaway kids. The people who were supposed to raise and love me instead discarded me. My ex-husband discarded me. It wasn't God.

The rejection, the hurt, and the pain I had gone through wasn't from God.

God was there with me the whole time, through the rejection, the hurt, and the pain. He never left me alone. When I wanted to die and end it all on many occasions, He (God) brought others into my life to revert my plans and the plans of the enemy. He showed that I mattered, that He cared for me in ways I couldn't fathom.

Also in His Word, Jeremiah 29:11 says, *"For I know the plans I have for you, declares the Lord. He has plans to prosper you and not to harm you, plans to give you hope and a future."* (NIV)

This scripture took me a while to accept. For the fact that God wouldn't harm me was what caught my attention. God was for me and not against me. Eventually, I hung tight to this scripture. I still do to this very day.

The one thing I know about Jesus is when He dealt with people here on earth, He dealt with people in love. He didn't reject people or beat people; nor did He curse at them. Jesus was all about love, healing, protection, deliverance, peace, mercy, and grace.

It was people who had rejected Jesus, as a matter of fact they were His people. They spit upon Him, beating Him savagely, to where it tore the skin off of Him all the way to the cross, yet He died for us, our sins, and all that ails us.

There is great freedom in Jesus. He is the lifeline, between us and Father God. Jesus didn't stay on the cross. When they buried Him, putting Him in the tomb, on the third day He rose. Jesus is alive and well. He will one day return for His people. I can't wait.

If we accept Him, we are forgiven, we have freedom, the shackles are broken off of us, and we have peace, joy, love, gentleness, kindness, mercy, patience, and so much more.

In Isaiah 26:3, it says, *"You will keep him in perfect peace, Whose mind is stayed on You."* (NKJV)

We can trust God; we can believe God and know God will do what He says He is going to do.

I spent many years not knowing my value and worth.

As I have said previously, our worth and value are not in what we do. It is in God.

By nature, I love helping others. That makes me feel good about myself. In any job, anytime I received an award I felt good about myself, but the moment I made a mistake, to me life was over, so to speak. In other words, I was striving to be a perfectionist. We are nonperfect. I have had a hard time when I am told I make a mistake. It is a huge stressor for me. I revert back to those lies that I am not good enough, or I will never amount to anything. I know this isn't true. Everyone makes mistakes. I know I will overcome this. I recall a few months back when I had gone up for prayer and one of the ministers prayed over me and said, "Your value is not in what you do. Your value is in God."

I had sat in a meeting about a month ago and something unkind was said. I was nearly in tears and God reminded me of that prayer.

The one thing I know God will redirect us. It is a daily fight. As T.D. Jakes says, "We are to be renewed by the transforming of our minds." (Romans 12:2, Ephesians 4:23)

Lamentations 3:22–23 talks about how God's mercies are new every morning.

Nehemiah 8:10 says, *"The joy of the Lord is your strength."*

God's Word is full of so much love, direction, declaration, words of comfort, peace, sincerity, and so much more. I know for myself as I speak God's Word into my own life. I receive abundant peace, strength, wisdom, knowledge, joy, and much more.

My worth isn't in what I was told as a child and in my marriage. As I previously stated, "Those were lies that I had believed." I choose to no longer to believe those lies.

God chose me for such a time as this.

God has brought me a mighty long way. He has not forsaken me. I no longer have to walk on eggshells. I don't have to worry about what someone will say or do to me. I felt this way about God. I never had to worry about this with God. Due to what I believed that was what I believed. God isn't out to punish me. God is an amazing, loving, kind God.

He is my father, my redeemer, my provider, my healer, my court advocate, and the list goes on. I will repeat this over and over. I want everyone to know God and who He is in your life.

www.ingramcontent.com/pod-product-compliance
Lightning Source LLC
Chambersburg PA
CBHW050642160426
43194CB00010B/1775